His Light in Our Darkness

✳ ✳ ✳

*

His Light in Our Darkness

* * *

AN ANTHOLOGY OF PRAISE

Fiona Castle

Hodder & Stoughton
LONDON   SYDNEY   AUCKLAND

British Library Cataloguing in Publication Data
A record for this book is available from
the British Library

ISBN 0 340 90833 5

Printed and bound in Great Britain by
Clays Ltd, St Ives plc

The paper used in this book is a natural recyclable
product made from wood grown in
sustainable forests. The hard
coverboard is recycled.

Hodder & Stoughton
A Division of Hodder Headline Ltd
338 Euston Road
London NW1 3BH
www.madaboutbooks.com
and www.hodderbibles.co.uk

Contents

✿ ✿ ✿

Acknowledgments

❋ ❋ ❋

While every effort has been made to contact the copyright holders of material used in this book, this has not always been successful. Full acknowledgment will gladly be made in future editions.

We gratefully acknowledge the following:

Eddie Askew, 'Lord, I'm Rich Because of Hope', excerpted from *A Silence and a Shouting* by Eddie Askew, copyright © 1982. Used by permission of The Leprosy Mission International, www.leprosymission.org. All rights reserved.

Eddie Askew, 'Lord, in the Quietness', excerpted from *Disguises of Love* by Eddie Askew, copyright © 1983. Used by permission of The Leprosy Mission International, www.leprosymission.org. All rights reserved.

Horatius Bonar, 'The Life Above', taken from the book *Longing for Heaven*. Used with permission of Christian Focus Publications.

Chris Bowater, 'Faithful God', copyright © 1990 Sovereign Lifestyle Music Ltd, sovereignmusic@aol.com.

Parent and reproduced by permission of Hodder & Stoughton Ltd.

Timothy Dudley-Smith, 'Tell Out My Soul': for Europe and Africa, copyright © Timothy Dudley-Smith; for the rest of the world including the USA and Canada, copyright © 1962, Ren. 1990 Hope Publishing Company. Used by permission.

Bob Gass, extracts from *The Word for Today*, used with permission from TWFT with copies available from United Christian Broadcasters, tel: 0845 60 40 401.

Dag Hammarskjöld, extract reprinted from *Markings* by Dag Hammarskjöld. Copyright © 1964. Used by permission of Faber & Faber.

Rob Hayward, extract taken from the song 'I'm Accepted, I'm Forgiven', copyright © 1985 Thankyou Music and administered by worshiptogether.com songs excl. UK & Europe, administered by Kingsway Music, tym@kingsway.co.uk. Used by permission.

Michael Hudson and Gary Diskell, 'I Want to Know Christ'. Copyright © Ariose Music. Unisong for Baltic States, Eastern Europe, Russia, Europe. Administered by Kevin Mayhew Ltd, UK & Eire (www.kevinmyhewltd.com).

Brenda Hunter, extract reprinted from *The Power of Mother Love*. Copyright © 1997 Brenda Hunter, Ph.D. WaterBrook Press, Colorado Springs, CO. All rights reserved.

Introduction

❈ ❈ ❈

*T*he purpose of this book is to focus on making our lives a blessing to God instead of always expecting him to bless us, living our lives thinking not of what we can get from God, but of what we can give him; a sacrifice of praise to him in all circumstances, realising that it is not our problems but how we respond to our problems which shapes our character.

It is better to be in a place of difficulty with the Lord, than anywhere else without him.

I came to this understanding many years ago when, at the age of thirty-five, I made the classic statement, 'There has to be more to life than this!'

Yet, I was a woman who, materially, had just about everything – a loving husband, a comfortable home, four beautiful, healthy children – outwardly fulfilled, yet empty on the inside.

When I arrived at this impasse, I confided in a Christian woman, Tamara, who suggested to me that the only solution to my dilemma would be to invite Jesus into my life as Lord and Saviour, so that my rather ritualistic and ineffectual 'religion' would become a relationship with the One who had paid the price, with his own life, to cancel my sin and give me the assurance, through my trust in him, of eternal life.

There is salvation in no one else. There is no other name in all of heaven for people to call on to save them.

Acts 4:12, NLT

What a transformation! God began to change my mind, my thinking, my attitude to all my circumstances. Although I dislike the connotations of the phrase – I had been born all over again!

God had set me on a pathway and I am still on that journey.

I echo the words of Paul.

I don't mean to say that I have already achieved these things or that I have already reached perfection! But I keep working towards that day when I will finally be all that Christ Jesus saved me for and wants me to be. No, dear brothers and sisters, I am still not all I should be, but I am focusing all my energies on this one thing: forgetting the past and looking forward to what lies ahead, I strain to reach the end of the race and receive the prize for which God, through Christ Jesus, is calling us up to heaven.

Philippians 3:12–14, NLT

So, this is a book not of sympathy but of rejoicing in our wonderful relationship with God – to help us draw closer to him and, as the song says, 'Praise Him in everything'.

Let my life be a love song to you, O Lord.

Come with me on a year's journey, as month by month we consider praising God through the different challenges of life.

Each chapter will not take a month to read! But perhaps as you ask God to speak to you, it will be an opportunity to pause, to contemplate and put into practice one aspect of change.

Take my life, and let it be

Take my life, and let it be
Consecrated, Lord, to Thee;
Take my moments and my days,
Let them flow in ceaseless praise.

Take my hands, and let them move
At the impulse of Thy love;
Take my feet, and let them be
Swift and beautiful for Thee.

Take my voice, and let me sing
Always, only, for my King;
Take my lips, and let them be
Filled with messages from Thee.

Take my silver and my gold,
Not a mite would I withhold;
Take my intellect, and use
Every power as Thou shalt choose.

Take my will, and make it Thine;
It shall be no longer mine:
Take my heart, it is Thine own;
It shall be Thy royal throne.

Take my love; my Lord, I pour
At Thy feet its treasure store:
Take myself, and I will be
Ever, only, all, for Thee.

Frances Ridley Havergal, 1836–74

*F*rances Ridley Havergal wrote this hymn in 1874 and this was a comment she made about it:

Consecration is not so much a step as a course; not so much an act, as a position to which a course of action inseparably belongs ...

We do not want to go on taking a first step over and over again. What we want now is, to be maintained in that position, and to fulfil that course.

January

***

*J*anuary is traditionally a time for making a new start – New Year's resolutions – and a time to let go of things past – old habits and grievances, which hold us back from becoming the 'new creation' God has in mind for us to be.

In the inimitable words of Oswald Chambers,

As we go forth into the coming year, let it not be in the haste of impetuous, unremembering delight, nor with the flight of impulsive thoughtlessness, but with the patient power of knowing that the God of Israel will go before us. Our yesterdays present irreparable things to us; it is true that we have lost opportunities which will never return, but God can transform this destructive anxiety into a constructive thoughtfulness for the future.

Let the past sleep, but let it sleep on the bosom of Christ.

Leave the irreparable past in His hands, and step out into the irresistible future with Him.

CHAPTER ONE

Take my life, and let it be

Consecrated, Lord, to Thee

✳ ✳ ✳

As a child, I loved to sing hymns. This one became a firm favourite when I learnt it at the boarding-school I attended from the age of nine.

I'm sure I didn't understand the reality of it at such a tender age, but in my innocence I really did mean the words I was singing. It was so much later when the full implications of allowing Jesus to 'take' my life became real.

> I plead with you to give your bodies to God. Let them be a living and holy sacrifice ... let God transform you into a new person by changing the way you think.
>
> *Romans 12:1–2, NLT*

We pray these words and we sing them but when God answers, we whine! 'Oh, I didn't mean that, Lord! I want everything to be right in my little world!' The verse before it in Romans 11 reminds us that 'everything comes from God and everything exists by His power and is intended for His glory'. God calls us to enter into his life and consecrate ourselves to him. To consecrate means 'to set apart as sacred'. Therefore, we have to put to death our selfish desires for life to go the way we want.

I know in this respect I have a long way to go because there's an awful lot of me that's still alive!

I have to start each day by consecrating myself to him afresh, praying I won't get in the way of his (not my) plans for the day.

Dying to self is a progressive journey and I have come to believe that it is only travelled through praise. The very act of praise releases the power of God into circumstances and enables God to work his purposes out through them.

Life is not a problem to be solved but a work
to be done.

Anon.

I want to worship the Lord with all of my heart
Give Him my all, not just a part;
Lift up my hands to the King of Kings
Praise Him in everything.

Robert Cameron

Jesus didn't promise to change the circumstances around us, but he did promise great peace and pure joy to those who would learn that God actually does control all things.

There is no pit so deep that Jesus is not deeper still.

Corrie ten Boom

Let your light so shine before men, that they may see your good works and glorify your Father in heaven.

Matthew 5:16, NKJV

What do you imagine people might think when they look at you?

Do they feel better for being with you? Are you trustworthy? Consistent? Are they attracted to Jesus through you?

We are known by our *fruits*, not by our lack of fungus or leaf rot!

Mark Buchanan

With eager heart and will on fire
I strove to win my great desire
'Peace shall be mine' I said, but life
Grew bitter in the barren strife.

Broken at last, I bowed my head
Forgetting all myself and said
'Whatever comes, His will be done'
And in that moment peace was won.

Henry Van Dyke, 1852–1933

*T*he peace Jesus gives is not dependent on our circumstances being peaceful.

Even the darkest hour lasts only sixty minutes.

Anon.

*W*e have to let Jesus help himself to our lives, serving not our own ends, but his. The disciples left everything to follow a man they didn't know and would never understand. They gave up the right to know where he would lead them, how much it would cost them and how much it would change them.

When Peter questioned Jesus about the lives of the other disciples, Jesus replied, 'What is that to you? You follow me' (John 21:22, NLT).

There are two things to do with the gospel:
believe it and behave it.

Anon.

If you want me to believe in your Redeemer,
you have to look a little more redeemed.

Friedrich Nietzsche, 1844–1900

I made a life-changing decision on 25 February 1975,
to give my life to God and allow Jesus to become
the centre of it. If the word 'allow' sounds condes-
cending to the Creator of the universe, it is because
before that moment I couldn't imagine losing control
of my destiny, so afraid was I of letting go of the reins
of my life to anyone.

I thought my life would fall apart. How simple it
should have been that this Creator God had a
creative plan for my life, because he made me and
understands me. Therefore he surely knows what's
best for me. But it took me years to discover the truth,
not realising how I was grieving him by choosing to
go my own way.

Look, I am standing at the door and I am
constantly knocking. If anyone hears me
calling him and opens the door, I will come
in and enjoy fellowship with him and he
with me.

Revelation 3:20

13

*S*o I did!
And He did!

> We can't experience fellowship with Christ
> when He is on the outside. And that's where
> He is, outside the door of our hearts, knock-
> ing and wanting to come in and have a
> relationship with us. Will we open it? Now
> picture yourself on the other side of the
> door, this time the door of Heaven. You
> knock and it does not open. You are ex-
> cluded forever. Or you knock and it opens
> wide. Christ welcomes you into His eternal
> home to live with Him forever. The first
> opening of the door is yours. The next is
> His.

Comment from NLT Touchpoint Bible
on salvation

*H*ave you ever been challenged by someone asking
you if you have been 'born again'? If so, the
possibility is that you would have run a mile!

I was asked the question in a different way ...
'Have you invited Jesus into your life?'

'No', was my stunned reply.

That was when my challenger explained the verses
above. The famous painting by Holman Hunt, of
Jesus, lantern in hand, knocking on a door with no
handle, illustrates the invitation Jesus makes to us all
to allow him to take up residence in our hearts; to be

*with us 'through all the changing scenes of life',
giving us his mind, rather than our own, on life's
circumstances.*

THE STRANGER

Who is this chippy
This hippy
This lippy young man from the sticks?

Who is this creature
This preacher
This teacher who's so full of tricks?

Who is this wheeler
This dealer
This healer who raises the dead?

Who is this stranger
This danger
This manger-born breaker of bread?

Who is this leader
This feeder
This pleader for justice and grace?

Who is this singer
This covenant bringer
This flinger of stars into space?

Who is this sower
This grower
This knower of all that I am?

Who is this mender
This sender
This tender redeemer, the Lamb?

Who is this Maker
This shaker
This breaker of death's final sting?

Who is this pastor
This forty day faster
This Pharisee blaster
This demon outcaster –

My Master
My God
and my King

Mike Hollow

The peace which followed that experience was immeasurable and has remained with me ever since that life-changing day.

My peace I leave with you, my peace I give to you. Not as the world gives do I give to you, so do not be troubled or afraid.

Jesus (John 14:27)

What a strength and spring of life, what hope and trust, what glad, unresting energy, is in this one thought, to serve Him who is 'my Lord', ever near me, ever looking on; seeing my intentions before He beholds my failures; knowing my desires before He sees my faults; cheering me to endeavour greater things, and yet accepting the least; inviting my poor service, and yet, above all, content with my poorer love. Let us try to realize this, whatsoever, wheresoever we be. The humblest and the simplest, the weakest and the most encumbered, may love Him not less than the busiest and strongest, the most gifted and laborious. If our heart be clear before Him; if He be to us our chief and sovereign choice, dear above all, and beyond all desired; then all else matters little. That which concerneth us He will perfect in stillness and in power.

H. E. Manning

We are never living, but only hoping to live; and, looking forward always to being happy, it is inevitable that we never are so.

Blaise Pascal, 1623–62

There is much in the story of Jesus I don't understand and can't explain. Why did God send his Son? Why did he choose to redeem mankind through his death? But although I have to accept it by faith, I believe it with all my heart.

OVERWHELMED BY CREATION

How many are your works, O LORD! In wisdom you made them all.

Psalm 104:24, NIV

One day in Hyde Park, London, author Frank Sheed was speaking about the remarkable order and design of the universe, when a heckler shouted, 'Even I could make a better universe than your God!' Unruffled, Sheed replied, 'I won't ask you to do that today, but would you mind making a rabbit just to establish credibility?'

Know what? If the earth was as small as the moon, its gravitation couldn't sustain our needs. On the other hand, if it was as large as Jupiter, its extreme gravitation would make human movement almost impossible. If we were as close to the sun as Venus, the heat would be unbearable; if we were as far away as Mars, every region would experience snow and ice nightly. If the oceans were half their size, we'd get only 25% of our present rainfall. If they were one-eighth larger, annual precipitation would increase 400% turning the earth into a vast, uninhabitable swamp. Water solidifies at 32 degrees Fahrenheit. But if the oceans were subject to that law, the amount of thawing in the Polar Regions wouldn't balance out and we'd all end up encased in ice. To prevent this catastrophe, God put salt in the sea to alter its freezing point. Not a bad day's work!

David said, 'How many are Your works, O LORD! In wisdom You made them all ... I will sing praise to my God as long as I live' (Ps. 104:24–33, NIV). If God's workmanship wouldn't make you want to stop and praise Him, what would?

Bob Gass

KING OF KINGS

King of Kings, majesty,
God of heaven living in me,
Gentle Saviour, closest friend,
Strong deliv'rer, beginning and end,
All within me falls at your throne.

> *Your majesty, I can but bow,*
> *I lay my all before you now.*
> *In royal robes I don't deserve*
> *I live to serve your majesty.*

Earth and heav'n worship you,
Love eternal, faithful and true,
Who bought the nations, ransomed souls,
Brought this sinner near to your throne;
All within me cries out in praise.

> *Your majesty, I can but bow,*
> *I lay my all before you now.*
> *In royal robes I don't deserve*
> *I live to serve your majesty,*
> *I live to serve your majesty.*

Jarrod Cooper

TEARS OF JOY

Assurance, joy, assurance, feeling, joy, peace.
God of Jesus Christ, my God and thy God.
'Thy God shall be my God.'
Forgotten of the world and of all except God.
He is only found in the ways taught in the Gospel.
The sublimity of the human soul.
'Just Father, the world has not known thee,
but I have known thee.'
Joy, joy, joy, tears of joy.

from Pascal's account of a dramatic mystical
experience; the writing, wrapped in parchment, was
kept sewn into his clothing

*B*laise Pascal (1623–62) was the French scientist,
mathematician and religious philosopher.

The life of faith is not a life of mounting up
with wings, but a life of walking and not
fainting.

Oswald Chambers, 1874–1917

Lord, in the quietness
I feel your love
washing over me.
Lifting the dust, cleansing the dirt.
I feel your hands, firm,
gentle, with the towel.
I can take that.
What I find hard, too hard to take,
is seeing you kneeling
at my feet.

I can understand, Peter.
I can feel his shock
as he looked down,
looked down on you.
To find you on the floor.
The protests rise in my throat,
as they did in his.
I can accept a high and mighty God,
It fits the pattern of the world I live in.
A world of yes sir, no sir,
three bags full sir.
But to see you, Lord,

there, at my feet. That's hard.
It makes me uncomfortable. I feel
      threatened.
It's too great a gift.
I want to lift you up
and put you back on the pedestal.
That's where God belongs.

And yet I think I see what you're saying.
That in a world where everything has to be
      paid for
your love is free.
That in your kingdom, privilege counts –
for nothing.
And that all the values of the world
turn upside down at your touch.
Lord, it's your gift.
It's so great,
so different from anything I've ever known,
It has no price tag.
I can't save for it, can't earn it,
Can't even bargain for it.
Just accept it.

Lord, give me the humility
to accept your humility.

Eddie Askew

W/hat prevents us from opening the door to Jesus?

Is it a desire to maintain independence?
Is it busyness?
It is pride?
Is it because of the assumption that
Christianity is only for weak people?
Is it because you think you're happy the
way you are?

The truth is that

> God has planted eternity in the human
> heart.

> *Ecclesiastes 3:11, NLT*

and that 'No one comes to the father except through
me' because 'I am the way, the truth and the life'
(Jesus), and while we refuse him access, our lives are
the poorer.

> So let us come boldly to the throne of our
> gracious God. There we will receive his
> mercy, and we will find grace to help us
> when we need it.

> *Hebrews 4:16, NLT*

If God had a refrigerator, your picture would be on it. If He'd a wallet, your photo would be in it. He sends you flowers every spring and a sunrise every morning. Whenever you want to talk, He'll listen. He can live anywhere in the universe, but He chose your heart. And what about the Christmas gift He sent you at Bethlehem? Not to mention that Friday at Calvary. Face it, He's crazy about you!

Max Lucado

When God begins to change our thinking, he challenges fears, insecurities and mindsets and helps us become all he has in mind for us to be.

A new appreciation and understanding of the Bible becomes evident as we begin to apply his teaching to our own lives.

There is always conflict between the 'old' life and the 'new' and nowhere is this more evident that in Paul's letter to the Galatians.

When you follow the desires of your sinful nature, your lives will produce these evil results: sexual immorality, impure thoughts, eagerness for lustful pleasure ... quarrelling, jealousy ... anger ...

But when the Holy Spirit controls our lives, he will produce this kind of fruit in us: love, joy, peace, patience, kindness, goodness, faithfulness, gentleness, and self control. Here there is no conflict with the law.

Galatians 5:19–23, NLT

You must put aside your selfish ambition, shoulder your cross and follow me. If you try to keep your life for yourself, you will lose it. But if you give up your life for my sake and for the sake of the Good News, you will find true life.

Mark 8:34–35, NLT

If we:

do whatever God commands however difficult;

endure whatever God appoints, however severe;

die daily to ourselves, however costly;

love our enemies, however misunderstood we may be;

pray without ceasing and always give thanks in everything

we shall know the blessing and joy of sacrifice.

Anon.

The measure of a life, after all, is not its duration, but its donation.

Corrie ten Boom

My life is but a weaving between my
     God and me,
I do not choose the colours, He works
     so steadily.
Oft' times He weaves in sorrow, and I
     in foolish pride,
Forget He sees the upper, and I the
     underside.

Not till the loom is silent, and the
     shuttles cease to fly
Will God unroll the canvas, and
     explain the reason why.
The dark threads are as needful in the
     Weaver's skilful hand
As the threads of gold and silver in the
     pattern He has planned.

Anon.

I was talking to a friend recently on the topic of praising God in all circumstances and he reminded me of the most important words in the Shorter Catechism:

'What is the chief end of man?'
'To glorify God and to enjoy him for ever.'

I confess I had totally forgotten those words! I learnt the whole catechism out of the Book of Common Prayer when I was confirmed at the age of eleven. We were tested on the words by the school chaplain and were not allowed to be confirmed unless we were word-perfect!

I reread those words after that conversation and realised that I believed everything in that catechism I had learned so long ago and appreciated it afresh. I became aware of the importance of the words of Peter, calling us to make every effort to apply the promises of God to our lives. We can read the words and we can believe them, but unless we apply them, they are useless.

I started to ponder on the words 'enjoy him for ever'. As I did, I began to smile. It was not a word I would ever have associated with my relationship with God; worship, yes; praise, yes; fear, yes, but enjoy? Now every time I repeat those words in my mind, my heart is warmed and I smile!

So, you see, it isn't enough just to have faith.

Faith that doesn't show itself by good deeds
is no faith at all – it is dead and useless.

James 2:17, NLT

And by that same mighty power, he has
given us all of his rich and wonderful
promises. He has promised that you will
escape the decadence all around you caused
by evil desires and that you will share in his
divine nature.

So make every effort to apply the benefits
of these promises to your life. Then your
faith will produce a life of moral excellence. A
life of moral excellence leads to knowing God
better. Knowing God leads to self-control.
Self-control leads to patient endurance and
patient endurance leads to godliness. Godliness leads to love for other Christians, and
finally you will grow to have genuine love for
everyone. The more you grow like this, the
more you will become productive and useful
in your knowledge of our Lord Jesus Christ.
But those who fail to develop these virtues
are blind or, at least, very shortsighted. They
have already forgotten that God has cleansed
them from their old life of sin.

So, dear brothers and sisters, work hard to
prove that you really are among those God
has called and chosen. Doing this, you will
never stumble or fall away. And God will
open wide the gates of heaven for you to

enter into the eternal Kingdom of our Lord
and Saviour Jesus Christ.

2 Peter 1:4–11, NLT

*Unless our actions are in harmony with our beliefs,
our words will be useless. We have to 'walk our
talk'.*

Crown Him with many crowns,
The Lamb upon His throne
Hark, how the heavenly anthem drowns
All music but its own!
Awake, my soul, and sing
Of Him who died for thee,
And hail Him as thy matchless King
Through all eternity.

Crown Him the Lord of life
Who triumphed o'er the grave
And rose victorious in the strife
For those He came to save:
His glories now we sing,
Who died and rose on high,
Who died eternal life to bring
And lives that death may die.

Crown Him the Lord of years,
The Potentate of time,
Creator of the rolling spheres,
Ineffably sublime!
All hail, Redeemer, hail!
For Thou hast died for me;
Thy praise shall never, never fail
Throughout eternity.

Matthew Bridges and Godfrey Thring

Questions to ponder

❀ ❀ ❀

1 *Have you consecrated your life to God?*
   or
   Is Jesus still knocking at the door of your heart? Will you let Him in?

2 *What is the Holy Spirit showing you in terms of change of attitude?*

3 *The Bible is God's handbook to life. Have you started to study it? Choose some Bible study notes at your local Christian bookshop to suit you and take them at your own pace.*

4 *Someone once said to me, 'Read the Bible until God speaks to you. That way you will be reading expectantly and be ready to listen and respond to what he is saying.'*

February

※ ※ ※

*F*ebruary can be a fairly bleak month – the weather, cold and drab; the promise of spring seems improbable, apart from the boldness of a few hardy snowdrops. Our immune systems are traditionally at their lowest, so that colds and worse are rife and we long for the warmth of the sun to revive us and re-ignite our spirits.

Sometimes, when we are on a long, tough walk, the going gets so difficult we daren't look further than the next painful step. If we look into the distance and see how far we still have to travel and how rough the terrain, we might be tempted to give up. Life can be like that … the pain is so great, we can hardly bear to look further than the next moment … we can only take one step at a time.

So, this month, let us focus on trusting God in the difficulty and pain of our circumstances, moment by moment, day by day.

CHAPTER TWO

Take my moments and my days

Let them flow in ceaseless praise

❊ ❊ ❊

He who loses gold or silver can find more to replace it, but he who loses time can never find more.

Fourth-century saying

Time is one of our most precious commodities. Each of us might be only one breath away from the end of it, yet we waste it, we fail to appreciate it, we regret its passing and some of us never have enough of it!

It is true to say that time goes more quickly with every passing year. I remember, as a small child, how long it took for birthdays to come around. Now they are almost tripping up over each other! I hear people in the shops saying, 'Is it really that time of year again? I've hardly got over last Christmas!'

Two things, which above all others, most want to be under strict rule and which are the greatest blessing to ourselves and others when they are rightly used, are our time and our money.

William Law, 1686–1761

Praise to the Lord, the Almighty, the
    King of creation!
O my soul, praise Him, for He is thy
    health and salvation!
All ye who hear,
Brothers and sisters, draw near,
Praise Him in glad adoration.

Praise to the Lord, who o'er all things so
    wonderfully reigneth,
Shelters thee under his wings, yea, so
    gently sustaineth.
Hast thou not seen –
All that is needful hath been
Granted in what he ordaineth.

Praise to the Lord, who dost prosper thy
    work and defend thee;
Surely His goodness and mercy here daily
    attend thee:
Ponder anew
What the Almighty can do,
Who with His love doth befriend thee.

Joachim Neander, 1650–80,
tr. Catherine Winkworth, 1829–78

I will praise you, my God and King,
    and bless your name for ever and ever
I will bless you every day,
    and I will praise you for ever
Great is the LORD! He is most worthy of
    praise!
His greatness is beyond discovery!
Let each generation tell its children of
    your mighty acts
I will meditate on your majestic, glorious
    splendour
and your wonderful miracles.
Your awe-inspiring deeds will be on every
    tongue;
I will proclaim your greatness.

Psalm 145:1– 6, NLT

I remember as a small child once (only once!),
whining to my mother that I was bored. 'Well, if
you're bored, go to bed', came her harsh and effective
reply! I can honestly say, from that time on, I have
never been bored. It was an impeccable lesson of
learning to find something to do in every circumstance
and to make the most of every moment.

Never delay
To do the duty which the hour brings
Whether it be in great or smaller things
For who doth know
What he shall do the coming day?

Anon.

As a mother, it was more a question of needing a few more hours in the day to accomplish all I had to do. A good lesson to remember is that God gives us enough time to accomplish what he wants us to do. If we are overstretched, what are we doing that he doesn't want us to do?

It takes less time to do a thing right than it does to explain why you did it wrong.

Henry Wadsworth Longfellow, 1807–82

Lord, if I am to be
My best for you
I must rest in you.
Lord, if I am to shine
For you, I must give
All that's mine to you,
My time to you.
Lord, if I am to show the way
To you, I must pray in you –
Give each day to you.
Lord, if I am to tell of you
I must dwell in you.
Lord, if I am to achieve
For you, I must receive from you.
Lord, please grant me grace,
Let me give you space.

Marilyn Dougan

To be in your presence
To sit at your feet
Where your love surrounds me
And makes me complete

This is my desire O Lord
This is my desire

To rest in your presence
Not rushing away
To cherish each moment
Here I would stay

This is my desire O Lord ...

Noel Richards

In thy hand it is.... To give strength
unto all.

Anon.

If our days are a constant rush and hurry
week in and week out, there is grave reason
to doubt if it is all God-given seed that we
are scattering. He will give us no more to do
than can be done with our spirits kept quiet
and ready and free before Him.

Lilias Trotter, 1853–1928

Children of God be men of rest – let every piece of work you do be touched with something of God's eternal rest. Let there be the calm of God upon you.

Anon.

Line upon line, here a little and there a little (Isa. 28:10). When the burdens of the day pile up in appalling confusion, think on this verse. Try something small first; go a short way at a time. You will be surprised how the work lessens like melting snow. Order will come out of confusion and peace will be yours in place of perturbation.

E. A. Needham

If our lives are to 'flow in ceaseless praise', we cannot pick and choose our moments to be spiritual and holy. God doesn't expect us to live in a vacuum or become reclusive. He longs to see our lives, in all circumstances, praising him. He knows our joys and pains, our highs and lows.

There was a time, before I became a Christian, when I felt lonely and totally devalued because my job description was that of housewife and mother. For me, it was more than full-time employment and yet there was no affirmation from society.

Later, God showed me that he had set me free to be what he wanted me to be, not what others expected me to be. Why should I worry what others thought of me? At that time he had entrusted me with a husband and four children. He wanted me to take that responsibility seriously and do a good job looking after them. My self-esteem soared.

Seeking God's will first brings perspective.

Proverbs 3:6

'Return to sender'. God has written a love letter to His world, but the world keeps sending it back unopened.

Revd Stephen Gaukroger

But although the world was made through him, the world didn't recognize him when he came ... But to all who believed him and accepted him, he gave the right to become children of God.

John 1:10–12, NLT

And he will give you everything you need from day to day if you live for him and make the Kingdom of God your primary concern.

Matthew 6:33, NLT

We only deliberately waste time with those
we love – it is the purest sign that we love
someone when we choose to spend time idly
in their presence when we could be doing
something more constructive.

Sheila Cassidy

*What a wonderful description of love! Isn't this
how we should feel about Jesus? We will, if we
put him first in our lives and spend time with him,
find out more about him and see how he led by
example.*
If not now, when?

If you spend your time waiting for the storm
to blow over, you'll never enjoy the
sunshine.

Anon.

Dost thou love life? Then do not squander
time, for that is the stuff life is made of.

Benjamin Franklin

Children spell love T.I.M.E.

Steve Chalke

*D*on't ever imagine there is a satisfactory substitute for giving time to your children.

Think of the influence we have on our children, or the influence our parents had on us. Is there anything that made more of a difference – not just for a moment, but for a lifetime? Which one of us doesn't carry some memory of words our parents said to us when we were young – words that hurt – or words that make us walk tall?

Those are the words we never forget, and they shape our image of who we are. If they hurt, we can spend much of our adult life trying to ease the pain. But if they gave us pride or confidence, it is that which will stay with us through the years. Tell your child you love her, you love him, and in that one act of letting them know they are loved, you give them the strength to love in return. I don't know of a greater gift; and all it takes is a few seconds of our time and our heart.

Professor Jonathan Sachs, Chief Rabbi

Surrendering to mother love, then, means giving your child your love, your time, and your attention when he needs it. It means choosing to live your life in such a way that you are physically present and emotionally available for large chunks of 'quantity' time, even when it's inconvenient. It means making difficult choices – professional, financial, and personal choices – so that you can be with your child in body, heart, mind and soul. It may mean postponing your dreams. It will definitely mean making sacrifices.

Brenda Hunter

Don't copy the behaviour and customs of this world, but let God transform you into a new person by changing the way you think.

Romans 12:2, NLT

In the newsletter of Full Time Mothers, an organisation which champions mothers at home, a contributor wrote:

Families these days simply cannot face taking a drop in income, when society puts so much emphasis on whether one has the 'right' clothes, new car, etc. ... Society needs to value the role of parenting over and above consumerism.

*A*nother wrote that when she gave up work her family income was so low that she qualified for free milk tokens, etc., and managed only because she made drastic cutbacks in spending. She went on:

> We need to value childhood and not regard babies as accessories that can easily be farmed out to enable life to get back to normal as quickly as possible. This seems to be the increasing trend. Is work (and money) really more important than sharing love and caring? If these are our values, should we be surprised if our children grow up to be selfish and materialistic?

*Y*ou cannot escape the responsibility of tomorrow by evading it today.

> My dishes went unwashed today,
> I didn't make the bed.
> I took his hand and followed
> Where his eager footsteps led.
>
> Oh yes, we went adventuring,
> My little son and I ...
> Exploring all the great outdoors
> Beneath the summer sky.
>
> We waded in a crystal stream,
> We wandered through a wood ...
> My kitchen wasn't swept today
> But life was gay and good.

We found a cool, sun-dappled glade
And now my small son knows
How Mother Bunny hides her nest,
Where jack-in-the pulpit grows.

We watched a robin feed her young,
We climbed a sunlit hill ...
Saw cloud-sheep scamper through
    the sky,
We plucked a daffodil.

That my house was neglected,
That I didn't brush the stairs,
In twenty years, no one on earth
Will know, or even care.

But that I've helped my little boy
To noble manhood grow,
In twenty years, the whole wide world
May look and see and know.

Anon.

*E*very time you say 'yes' to someone else, you are
saying 'no' to your children.

There will never be a more worthwhile and valuable
job to do than bringing up the next generation of secure
adults. An awesome responsibility!

If you have a high-flying job and are made re-
dundant you will be forgotten in a week, but what
you do for your children will be remembered long after
they have flown the nest.

Every moment of our sacrificial time is a song of praise to the Lord.

If you said, 'That'll do' at the completion of a task, it generally means you could have done it better!

> With Jesus' help, let us continually offer our sacrifice of praise to God by proclaiming the glory of his name. Don't forget to do good and to share what you have with those in need, for such sacrifices are very pleasing to God.

Hebrews 13:15–16, NLT

LIFE IS 'SHORT AND SWEET'

'I'd eat more ice cream and laugh more', was the rather surprising reply of a senior and somewhat stern lawyer, with a reputation for working very long hours, when asked what she'd do differently if she had her years over again. 'I'd ride more rollercoasters', she continued, 'sing louder in the bath, stay up late more often watching films with my friends, and spend a *lot* more time with my children!'

It's too easy to get trapped into living life on the basis that, though it's just one long hard slog today, one day it'll be easier and the slog will suddenly prove to have all been worth it. But the truth is, that day may never come.

Steve Chalke

SLOW DANCE

Have you ever watched kids
On a merry-go-round?
Or listened to the rain
Slapping on the ground?
Ever followed a butterfly's erratic flight?
Or gazed at the sun into the fading night?
You'd better slow down.
Don't dance so fast.
Time is short.
The music won't last.
Do you run through each day
On the fly?
When you ask How are you?
Do you hear the reply?
When the day is done
Do you lie in your bed
With the next hundred chores
Running through your head?
You'd better slow down
Don't dance so fast.
Time is short.
The music won't last.
Ever told your child,
We'll do it tomorrow?
And in your haste,
Not see his sorrow?
Ever lost touch,
Let a good friendship die
Cause you never had time
To call and say, 'hi'
You'd better slow down.

Don't dance so fast.
Time is short.
The music won't last.
When you run so fast to get somewhere
You miss half the fun of getting there.
When you worry and hurry through your day,
It is like an unopened gift ...
Thrown away.
Life is not a race.
Do take it slower
Hear the music
Before the song is over.

Colin and Jill MacRae

FOR THE BEAUTY OF THE EARTH

For the beauty of the earth,
For the beauty of the skies,
For the love which from our birth
Over and around us lies,
Father, unto thee we raise
This our sacrifice of praise.

For the beauty of each hour
Of the day and of the night,
Hill and vale and tree and flower,
Sun and moon and stars of light,
Father, unto thee we raise
This our sacrifice of praise.

For the joy of ear and eye,
For the heart and mind's delight,
For the mystic harmony
Linking sense to sound and sight,
Father, unto thee we raise
This our sacrifice of praise.

For the joy of human love
Brother, sister, parent, child,
Friends of earth, and friends above,
For all gentle thoughts and mild,
Father, unto thee we raise
This our sacrifice of praise.

For each perfect gift of thine
To our race so freely given,
Graces human and divine,
Flowers of earth and buds of Heaven,
Father, unto thee we raise
This our sacrifice of praise.

Folliot Sandford Pierpoint, 1835–1917

LORD, remind me how brief my time on earth
    will be.
Remind me that my days are numbered, and
    that my life is fleeing away.
My life is no longer than the width of my
    hand.
An entire lifetime is just a moment to you;
human existence is but a breath.

Psalm 39:4–5, NLT

Questions to ponder

❊ ❊ ❊

1 *Are you making the best use of your time? If not, what can you change that would make a difference?*

2 *If you have children, what can you do to maximise your time with them? (Remember 'quality' time is no good without 'quantity' time!)*

3 *It has been said that if you are too busy to spend time with God each day, you are busier than God intends you to be. He enables us to fulfil the work he has given us to do. Are you too busy?*

4 *Does what you're doing have eternal value? If you knew this year would be your last year on earth, how would you reorganise your priorities?*

March

Spring is on its way! The days are getting longer and nature provides evidence of all things new. For those privileged to have gardens, busy hands will be preparing flowerbeds and nurturing seeds to plant in the vegetable patch. Traditionally 'spring-cleaning' takes place in the home, allowing the fresh air through the window and the sunlight to show up the dust!

As we consider the next verse from the hymn, perhaps we can ask the Lord to show us afresh how we can use our hands and our energy to benefit others.

CHAPTER THREE

Take my hands, and let them move

At the impulse of Thy love

* * *

Christ has no body now but yours,
No hands, no feet, on earth but yours.

Yours are the eyes through which he looks
With compassion on this world.

Yours are the feet
With which he walks to do good.

Yours are the hands
With which he blesses all the world.

Yours are the hands, yours are the feet
Yours are the eyes, you are his body.

Christ has no body now but yours,
No hands, no feet on earth but yours.
Yours are the eyes, through which he
        looks with compassion on the world.
Christ has no body now on earth but
        yours.

Attributed to St Thérèse of Lisieux, 1873–97

Do all the good you can
By all the means you can
In all the ways you can
In all the places you can
To all the people you can
As long as you ever can.

John Wesley, 1703–91

I realised my vocation when I first felt my heart beat with passion for the unloved in Calcutta.

Mother Teresa of Calcutta, 1910–97

The greatest love is shown when people lay down their lives for their friends.

John 15:13, NLT

For mercy has a human heart
Pity, a human face
And love the human form divine
And peace the human dress.

William Blake, 1757–1827

*U*nderstand that God isn't calling everyone to do *what you do. He is not asking everyone to endure what he has allowed you to endure. He is working in each of our lives differently, in amazing ways, so that, grateful for our uniqueness, we can always glorify the name of Jesus.*

No act of kindness, however small, is ever wasted.

Thank God every morning when you get up that you have something to do which must be done, whether you like it or not. Being forced to work and forced to do your best will breed in you temperance, self-control, diligence, strength of will, content and a hundred other virtues which the idle never know.

Charles Kingsley, 1819–75

Praise God in his heavenly dwelling;
praise him in his mighty heaven!
Praise him for his mighty works;
praise his unequalled greatness!
Praise him with a blast of the trumpet;
praise him with the lyre and harp!
Praise him with the tambourine and dancing;
praise him with stringed instruments and flutes!
Praise him with the clash of cymbals;
praise him with loud clanging cymbals.
Let everything that lives sing praises to the LORD.
Praise the LORD.

Psalm 150, NLT

As a young wife and mother, I worked myself to a frazzle trying to achieve perfection. I needed to be affirmed and applauded to survive. In spite of all this striving, my self-esteem remained at rock bottom. I was a perfectionist and perfectionists always see themselves as failures because they never match up to their own expectations of what perfection should be. This often makes the people around them miserable too.

Jesus changed all that. He challenged my mindset, my fears and insecurities and showed me that everything I did I should do 'as unto Him', however menial, unnoticed and seemingly insignificant the task; above all, performing each task with love, maintaining a happy atmosphere in the home.

I'm accepted, I'm forgiven,
I am fathered by the true and living God,
I'm accepted, no condemnation,
I am loved by the true and living God.
There's no guilt or fear as I draw near
to the Saviour and Creator of the world.
There is joy and peace as I release
my worship to You, O Lord.

Rob Hayward

I have noticed that wherever there has been a faithful following of the Lord in a consecrated soul, several things have inevitably followed, sooner or later. Meekness and quietness of spirit become in time the characteristics of the daily life. A submissive acceptance of the will of God as it comes in the hourly events of each day; pliability in the hands of God to do or to suffer all the good pleasure of his will; sweetness under provocation; calmness in the midst of turmoil and bustle; yieldingness to the wishes of others, and an insensibility to slights and affronts; absence of worry or anxiety; deliverance from care and fear – all these, and many similar graces, are invariably found to be the natural outward development of that inward life which is hid with Christ in God.

H. W. S.

It is only possible to be humiliated when we are serving our own pride.

Oswald Chambers, 1874–1917

'DO NOT WITHHOLD GOOD FROM THOSE WHO DESERVE IT ...'

Charles Plumb was a Navy pilot in Vietnam. After 75 missions his plane was destroyed and he parachuted into enemy territory. He survived 6 years in a communist prison. Now he lectures on his experiences. One day, a man came up to him and said, 'You're Plumb! You flew jet fighters from the aircraft carrier *Kitty Hawk*. You were shot down!' Plumb replied, 'How in the world did you know that?' Smiling, the man said, 'I packed your parachute. I guess it worked!'

That night Plumb couldn't sleep. He said, 'I kept wondering what that man might have looked like in uniform. How many times I'd walked past him without speaking, because I was a fighter pilot and he was just a sailor. I thought of the hours he'd spent in the bowels of the ship, carefully weaving the shrouds and folding the silks of each parachute, holding in his hands the fate of someone he didn't even know.'

So, who packed your parachute? Who helped you to get to where you are? Put their all on the line for you? Paul looks back and recalls people most of us have never heard of – like Priscilla and Aquila, '... who for my sake risked their necks' (Romans 16:4 NAS). There are no 'self-made' people. The higher you go, the more dependent you become on others. George Matthew Adams says, 'Everyone who

has ever done a kind deed or spoken a word of
encouragement ... has entered into the make-
up of our character ... our thoughts ... our
success.' So, who packed your parachute? Be
sure to show your appreciation!

Bob Gass

Able to suffer without complaining
To be misunderstood without explaining
Able to give without receiving
To be ignored without grieving
Able to ask without commanding
To love despite misunderstanding
Able to turn to the Lord for guarding
Able to wait for his own rewarding.

Anon.

LOVE

It has hands to help others
It has feet to hasten to the poor and needy
It has eyes to see misery and want
It has ears to hear the sighs and sorrows of men
That is what love looks like.

St Augustine of Hippo, 354–430

Perfect valour consists in doing without witnesses that which one would be capable of doing before everyone.

François, sixth Duc de La Rochefoucauld, 1613–80

Real generosity is doing something nice for someone who will never know your secret.

Anon.

The most excellent method Brother Lawrence had found of going to God was that of doing our common business without any view of pleasing men, and (as far as we are capable) purely for the love of God. Brother Lawrence stated:

* That it was a great delusion to think that the times of prayer ought to differ from other times; that we are as strictly obliged to adhere to God by action in the time of action as by prayer in its season.

* That his prayer was nothing else but a sense of the presence of God, his soul being at that time insensible to everything but divine love; and that when the appointed times of prayer were past he found no difference because he still continued with God, praising and

blessing him with all his might, so that he passed his life in continual joy; yet hoped that God would give him somewhat to suffer when he should grow stronger.

* That we ought, once for all, heartily to put our whole trust in God, and make a total surrender of ourselves to him, secure that he would not deceive us.

* That we ought not to be weary of doing little things for the love of God, who regards not the greatness of the work, but the love with which it is performed. That we should not wonder if in the beginning we often failed in our endeavours, but that at last we should gain a habit which will naturally produce its acts in us without our care and to our exceeding great delight.

Divine services conducted here three times a day.

A plaque by Ruth Bell Graham's kitchen sink!

W̶e don't mind being servants until we're treated like one!

But when the Son of Man comes in his glory, and all the angels with him, then he will sit upon his glorious throne. all the nations will be gathered in his presence, and he will separate them as a shepherd separates the sheep from the goats. He will place the sheep at his right hand and the goats at his left. Then the King will say to those on the right, 'Come you who are blessed by my Father, inherit the Kingdom prepared for you from the foundation of the world. For I was hungry, and you fed me. I was thirsty, and you gave me a drink. I was a stranger, and you invited me into your home. I was naked, and you gave me clothing. I was sick, and you cared for me. I was in prison, and you visited me.'

Then these righteous ones will reply, 'Lord, when did we ever see you hungry and feed you? Or thirsty and give you something to drink? Or a stranger and show you hospitality? Or naked and give you clothing? When did we ever see you sick or in prison and visit you? And the King will tell them, 'I assure you, when you did it to one of the least of these my brothers and sisters, you were doing it to me!'

Matthew 25:31–40, NLT

I was very impressed recently by a book written by Matt Roper about his experiences working with child prostitutes and street children in Brazil. It beautifully illustrates the passage above.

THE SCENT OF WATER

Just as Jesus touched the lepers and welcomed the outcasts, so must we. Just as He identified with the poor and the weak, so must we. He calls us to put our lives on the line for the suffering, the vulnerable, the victims of injustice. Loving the unloved is not just an optional extra. It is the heart and soul of the Christian gospel.

Jesus did not mince words, yet even today many of His followers fail to understand. 'Whatever you do for the least of these, you do for me,' He said. He is saying that, if we claim to love Him, we have to love them, the despised and downtrodden. To do this is not just to obey Christ. It is to minister to Christ Himself.

To each of us who profess to serve Him, Jesus looks us in the eyes and asks, 'How much do you love me? You say that you love me, you sing that you love me. But how much do you really love me? For I am out there on the streets, lost and lonely, lying in the gutter. I am being beaten and abused, robbed of my childhood. I am selling my body on the street corner, I am locked in a brothel bedroom. I am violent, despised, disposable. Do you really love me as much as you say? Then prove it.'

Job 14:7 tells us that when a tree is cut down, there is always hope that it will sprout again and produce new branches: 'Its roots may grow old in the ground and its stump die in the soil, yet at the scent of water it will bud and put forth shoots like a plant.' We need to be that 'scent of water', bringing hope and life, the life of Christ, to a dying world.

Matt Roper

He giveth more grace when the burdens
     grow greater
He sendeth more strength when the labours
     increase
To added afflictions He addeth His mercies
To multiplied trials, His multiplied peace.

When we have exhausted our store of
     endurance
When our strength has failed ere the day is
     half done
When we reach the end of our hoarded
     resources
Our Father's full giving is only begun.

His love has no limit, His grace has no
    measure
His power has no boundary known unto
    men
For out of His infinite riches in Jesus
He giveth and giveth and giveth again.

Annie Johnson Flint

Some people create happiness wherever they go. Others leave happiness whenever they go!

If you learn to laugh at your troubles, you'll always have something to laugh at.

Recently I made several trips to the Far East to visit some of the projects supported by Global Care, a charity caring for children at risk (of which I am a patron). I was also involved with making a video for the purpose of showing the sponsors that their money really was making a difference and that lives were being transformed as a result.

I confess I was a reluctant traveller. God had to shake me out of my comfort zone by showing me that if by going, life could be made better for even one child, I had no right to sit back and do nothing.

The following is a short extract from a diary I wrote en route:

As I set off for yet another trip abroad, the words of Annie Johnson Flint's poem [above] were on my lips.

As we reach the end of our hoarded
resources
Our Father's full giving is only begun.

*I began to see a parallel between those words
and the way I was feeling. I was travelling
alone, on a long-haul flight, to an unknown
(to me) destination and yet there was
immense joy welling up in me. Why was this?
After all, I was leaving behind the ones I
loved most in the world. An hour before I
had been rushing around trying to tie up
unfinished business, wondering if had given
myself enough time to get to Heathrow, given
the traffic on the M25.*

*Sitting in the departure lounge, I realised
there was nothing more I could physically do.
I was beyond the point of no return. All I
could do was to trust the One who gave me
life, new life and eternal life. I was in His
hands. Why should I be afraid?*

God is our refuge and strength,
always ready to help in times of trouble.
So we will not fear ...

Psalm 46:1–2, NLT

We have to let Jesus help Himself to our lives, serving not our own ends but His.

> And oft, when in my heart was heard
> Thy timely mandate I deferred
> The task, in smoother walks to stray;
> But thee I now would serve more
>   strictly if I may.

William Wordsworth, 1770–1850

My God, I choose the whole lot. No point in becoming a saint by halves. I'm not afraid of suffering for your sake; the only thing I'm afraid of is clinging to my own will. Take it; I want the whole lot; everything whatsoever that is your will for me.

St Thérèse of Lisieux, 1873–97

> Faithful God
> All sufficient one, I worship you
> Shalom my peace
> My strong Deliverer
> I lift you up
> Faithful God.

Chris Bowater

WHEN WE WALK WITH THE LORD
(TRUST AND OBEY)

When we walk with the Lord
In the light of His word,
What a glory He sheds on our way!
While we do His good will,
He abides with us still,
And with all who will trust and obey.

Trust and obey,
For there's no other way
To be happy in Jesus,
But to trust and obey.

Not a shadow can rise,
Not a cloud in the skies,
But his smile quickly drives it away;
Not a doubt nor a fear,
Not a sigh nor a tear,
Can abide while we trust and obey.

Trust and obey …

Not a burden we bear,
Not a sorrow we share,
But our toil He doth richly repay;
Not a grief nor a loss,
Not a frown nor a cross,
But is blest if we trust and obey.

Trust and obey …

But we never can prove
The delights of His love,
Until all on the altar we lay;
For the favour He shows,
And the joy He bestows
Are for them who will trust and obey.

Trust and obey …

Then in fellowship sweet,
We will sit at his feet,
Or we'll walk by His side in the way.
What He says we will do,
Where He sends we will go,
Never fear, only trust and obey.

Trust and obey …

John Henry Sammis, 1846–1919

Questions to ponder

* * *

1 Do you have an attitude of gratitude? Or are you always complaining?

2 Does your attitude colour your behaviour each day?

3 How can you begin to change this?

4 Write a list of your reasons to be grateful (e.g. do you have enough clothing, food, work?). Compare your life with some you read about in the developing world. Try to imagine living for one day in 'the shoes' of someone who has no shoes.

5 What can you do in the coming week to bless someone? How can you make a difference to their life?

6 Can you live in peace and contentment without coveting what others have and trusting God in your circumstances?

April

*A*pril is the month of the London Marathon! Tens of thousands gather at two locations to run the 26.3 miles round the well-marked route.

There are many different reasons for running a marathon. For some it will be to aim to be first across the finishing line, or to better their personal best. For others it will be the triumph of overcoming an illness or disability; but for the majority it will be in order to raise money for the benefit of others. For every entrant it takes the discipline of months – if not years – of training, a lot of energy and steely determination!

Isn't that a lot like life? Because we are all created differently, we have diverse purposes, plans, limitations and paces and, for some, survival is the best that can be hoped for.

The writer to the Hebrews tells us to 'Run with endurance the race that God has set before us. We do this by keeping our eyes on Jesus' (Heb. 12:1–2, NLT) and Paul said, 'I run straight to the goal with purpose in every step' (1 Cor. 9:26, NLT).

CHAPTER FOUR

Take my feet, and let them be

Swift and beautiful for Thee

❊ ❊ ❊

*A*s a former professional dancer, these words could have a literal meaning for me. As with most dancers, the love of dance and movement was born in me and was and still is always longing to express itself. There is nothing more releasing for me than to leap and dance on a deserted beach in the early morning!

I remember, as a student at school, a friend telling me she always danced for her Maker. It had an amazing impact on me. It gave me a new dimension to dance and a new inspiration to do my very best, even in rather uninspired classes!

> *Teach me to dance to the beat of Your heart,*
> *teach me to move in the power of Your spirit,*
> *teach me to walk in the light of Your presence,*
> *teach me to dance to the beat of Your heart.*
> *Teach me to love with Your heart of compassion,*
> *teach me to trust in the word of Your promise,*
> *teach me to hope in the day of Your coming,*
> *teach me to dance to the beat of Your heart*

You wrote the rhythm of life,
created Heaven and earth;
in You is joy without measure.
So like a child in Your sight
I dance to see Your delight
For I was made for your pleasure, pleasure.

Teach me to dance ...

Let all my movements express
a heart that loves to say 'yes',
a will that leaps to obey You.
Let all my energy blaze
to see the joy in Your face,
let my whole being praise You, praise You.

Teach me to dance ...

Graham Kendrick

*M*any years ago, at the tender age of seventeen, when I launched myself into my rather inauspicious career in show business, my dear father took me aside in one of those rare father–daughter moments, to share a pearl of wisdom from his own experience. 'Don't be afraid of adventure', he said, 'and don't allow fear to prevent you from doing anything. I was always afraid to step out into something new, and now I live with regrets that I lacked courage. I don't want you to live with regrets.'

These were unexpected words from a man who

had fought in the First World War, who had given his life for his patients as a general practitioner. In those days, before the NHS, the doctor was on call twenty-four hours a day, at the beck and call of his patients. He served them lovingly and willingly, charging them little and many times nothing at all when he knew circumstances were hard for them. I remember him saying that he never had much money, but because his own needs were few, he always had enough.

No one could say he had missed his way in life. He was loved and appreciated by his patients and his family. To me he was a giant of a man, to be respected and obeyed, and yet in this very special moment he was admitting a 'longing' that had never occurred to me.

I accepted it and stored what he had said in the archives of my mind for decades, airing it fleetingly to remind myself of it as I passed through various phases of family life before putting it away again.

I think it has only been in the past decade, as I have had to make many changes, returning to single-ness, that I have really understood what he was trying to tell me. The greatest mistake a person can make is to be afraid of making one.

John Ortberg, in his book If You Want to Walk on the Water, You've Got to Get Out of the Boat, *says this:*

> I believe there is something – Someone – inside us who tells us there is more to life than sitting in the boat. You were made for something more than merely avoiding failure. There is something inside you that wants to

walk on the water – to leave the comfort of routine existence and abandon yourself to the high adventure of following God.

So let me ask you a very important question: What's your boat?

Your boat is whatever represents safety and security to you apart from God himself. Your boat is whatever you are tempted to put your trust in, especially when life gets a little stormy. Your boat is whatever keeps you so comfortable that you don't want to give it up even if it's keeping you from joining Jesus on the waves. Your boat is whatever pulls you away from the high adventure of extreme discipleship.

Want to know what your boat is? Your fear will tell you. Just ask yourself this: what is it that most produces fear in me – especially when I think of leaving it behind and stepping out in faith?

Consider the postage stamp. It sticks to the package till it gets there.

Anon.

Throughout this toilsome world, alas!
Once and only once I pass
If a kindness I may show
If a good deed I may do
To a suffering fellow man
Let me do it while I can
No delay, for it is plain
I shall not pass this way again.

Anon.

He walked by faith and not by sight
By love and not by law
The presence of the wrong or right
He rather felt than saw.

J. G. Whittier

O Lord, this is our desire, to walk along the path of life that you have appointed us; in steadfastness of faith, in lowliness of heart, in gentleness of love.

Maria Hare, 1798–1870

*I*f we are truly set free in Jesus, we are not afraid of taking risks. Everything we do is risky. Nothing, anywhere guarantees us total safety. We can eat the right foods, take the right exercise, live a stress-free life, go to bed early, mind our own business and still slip on a banana skin!

Think big, or stay small.

Don't minimise risk; maximise opportunity.

Anon.

*M*y husband had an adventurous spirit. He took every opportunity presented to him. For the television series Record Breakers, he wing-walked, parachuted, parascended, did the longest death slide and more. When he was dying of cancer, he said he was so glad he had risen to the challenge to do all those things, because on coming to the end of his life, he had no regrets.

Refuse to let the word 'impossible' stop you. With God all things are possible (Matt. 19:26). If the people who've changed the world had left every impossible task undone, we'd still be living in the Dark Ages!

Where there is no vision, the people perish.

Proverbs 29:18

*A*fter Roy died, God called me to rise to the challenge too, in very different ways. He was showing me opportunities that were way out of my comfort zone. But what if I failed? It is only my pride that would be pricked!

My favourite definition of success is: 'getting up and getting going one more time than you've failed'.

> *All that I am I lay before You;*
> *all I possess, Lord, I confess*
> *is nothing without You.*
> *Saviour and King, I now enthrone You;*
> *take my life, my living sacrifice to You.*

> Lord, be the strength within my weakness;
> be the supply in every need,
> that I may prove Your promises to me,
> faithful and true in word and deed.

> *All that I am …*

> Into Your hands I place the future;
> the past is nailed to Calvary,
> that I may live in resurrection power,
> no longer I, but Christ in me.

> *All that I am …*

> *James Wright*

To laugh is to risk appearing a fool.

To weep is to risk appearing sentimental.

To reach out to another is to risk involvement.

To expose your feelings is to risk rejection.

To place your dreams before the crowd is to risk ridicule.

To love is to risk not being loved in return.

To go forward in the face of overwhelming odds is to risk failure.

But risks must be taken, because the greatest risk of all is to risk nothing.

The person who risks nothing, does nothing, has nothing and is nothing.

He may avoid suffering and sorrow, but he cannot learn, he cannot feel, he cannot change, he cannot grow and he cannot love. Chained by his certitudes, he is a slave. Only the person who risks is truly free.

Ask God for clarity to hear His voice, the wisdom to understand what He is saying to you and the courage to rise up and do it!

Bob Gass

*R*oy used to say that God has a big video camera in the sky and he's recording everything we do. One day we will have to sit with him and he will play back to us everything we have said and done on this earth! How sad to be wondering what would have happened if ... and if only ...

Don't live with regrets!

What can you do today to minimise the regret factor? It's not too late to make a start ...

> For we must all stand before Christ to be judged. We will each receive whatever we deserve for the good or evil we have done in our bodies.
>
> *2 Corinthians 5:10, NLT*

*Y*ou won't be rewarded for the 'well said', you'll be rewarded for the 'well done'. The risk of riskless living is the greatest risk of all. Don't end your life wishing you'd stepped out and followed God. Go ahead and do it!

> Earth's crammed with heaven
> And every common bush afire with God
> But only He who sees it takes off his shoes
> The rest sit round it and pick blackberries.
>
> *Elizabeth Barrett Browning, 1806–61*

THE COMMON COLD OF THE SOUL

To sinful patterns of the behaviour that
      never get confronted or changed,
Abilities and gifts that never get cultivated or
      deployed –
Until weeks become months
And months turn into years,
And one day you're looking back on a life of
Deep, intimate, gut-wrenchingly honest
      conversations
You have never had;
Great bold prayers you never prayed,
Exhilarating risks you never took,
Sacrificial gifts you never offered
Lives you never touched,
And you're sitting in a recliner with a
      shrivelled soul,
And forgotten dreams,
And you realise there was a world of
      desperate need,
And a great God calling you to be part of
      something bigger than yourself –
You see the person you could have become
      but did not;
You never followed your calling.
You never got out of the boat.

Gregg Levoy, Callings

The price one pays for pursuing any calling is an intimate knowledge of its ugly side.

Anon.

QUIET TIME

Forgive us, Lord, for snacking at Your feast, nibbling at righteousness, picking at Your promises, and showing up at Your table when we have time. If we, Your own, are undernourished by choice, how can we expect to feed a lost and hungry world?

Susan L. Lenzkes

Let us strip off every weight that slows us down, especially the sin that so easily hinders our progress.

Hebrews 12:1, NLT

Some men see things as they are and say 'why?' I dream things as they have never been and say 'why not?'

Anon.

Perhaps we all need to ask ourselves are we running away from where the real need is? Are we sticking to 'safe places' instead of moving beyond the gates to the front line of Christian mission and service? There can never be 'no-go zones' for those who walk with Jesus. He calls us to leave the safety of our Christian enclaves to be with those who are isolated and alienated, to serve those we fear, to speak for those who have no voice. To puncture our protective bubble of 'safe space' and stand with the powerless. Let's hear the call of Jesus to 'go into ALL the world'. Quite a challenge!

Rob Frost

A pessimist sees the difficulty in every opportunity; an optimist sees the opportunity in every difficulty.

Winston Churchill, 1874–1965

The Lord is my Helper and I am not afraid of anything that mere man can do to me.

Hebrews 13:6, LB

*T*he man who removes a mountain begins with moving small stones.

THINGS GOD WON'T ASK

God won't ask what kind of car you
drove, but will ask how many people
you drove who didn't have transportation.

God won't ask the square footage of
your house, but will ask how
many people you welcomed into
your home.

God won't ask about the fancy
clothes you had in your closet, but
will ask how many of those
clothes helped the needy.

God won't ask about your social
status, but will ask what kind of
class you displayed.

God won't ask how many material
possessions you had, but will ask
if they dictated your life.

God won't ask what your highest
salary was, but will ask if you
compromised your character to
obtain that salary.

God won't ask how much overtime you
worked, but will ask if you
worked overtime for your family
and loved ones.

God won't ask how many promotions
you received, but will ask how
you promoted others.

God won't ask what your job title
was, but will ask if you
performed your job to the best of your
ability.

God won't ask what you did to help
yourself, but will ask what you
did to help others.

God won't ask how many friends you
had, but will ask how many
people to whom you were
a true friend.

God won't ask what you did to
protect your rights, but will ask
what you did to protect the rights of
others.

God won't ask in what neighbourhood
you lived, but will ask how you
treated your neighbours.

God won't ask about the colour of
your skin, but will ask about the
content of your character.

God won't ask how many times your
deeds matched your words, but
will ask how many times they didn't.

When there is nothing left but God,
that is when you find out God is all you
need.

Anon.

I danced in the morning
When the world was begun,
And I danced in the moon
And the stars and the sun
And I came down from heaven
And I danced on the earth –
At Bethlehem I had my birth.

Dance, then, wherever you may be;
I am the Lord of the Dance, said he,
I'll lead you all, wherever you may be,
I will lead you all in the Dance, said he.

I danced for the scribe
And the Pharisee,
But they would not dance
And they couldn't follow me;
I danced for the fishermen,
For James and John –
They came with me
And the dance went on.

Dance, then ...

I danced on the Sabbath
And I cured the lame;
The holy people
Said it was a shame;
They whipped and they stripped
And they hung me high,
And they left me there
On a Cross to die.

Dance, then ...

I danced on a Friday
When the sky turned black –
It's hard to dance
With the devil on your back;
They buried my body
And they thought I'd gone –
But I am the dance
And I still go on.

Dance, then ...

They cut me down
And I leapt up high –
I am the life
That'll never, never die;
I'll live in you
If you'll live in me –
I am the Lord
Of the Dance, said he.

Dance, then ...

Sydney Carter

Questions to ponder

❋ ❋ ❋

1 What is preventing you from getting out of your comfort zone and taking risks for God?

2 Is it fear?

3 Is it fear of failure?
   What challenge is God calling you to take up?

4 Refusing to take risks doesn't guarantee us safety. If the safest place to be is in the centre of God's will, where is that place for you?

5 What makes you afraid to take up a new challenge?

6 What can you do today to minimise the regret factor at the end of your life?

May

*M*ay, it could be said, is the most beautiful month of the year.

The young foliage on the trees provides a fresh and vibrant variety of colours, while the blossom on the fruit trees offers the promise of the fruit we are so privileged to enjoy later in the year.

The scent of the azaleas fills the air with fragrance. All of these awaken our senses to the wonder of nature and God's abundant provision for us.

I remember walking alone through the forested mountains of Switzerland, marvelling at the beauty of the scenery. Some days I would not meet another soul all day, which gave me the courage to sing in the way I would dance on a deserted beach – in praise of my Maker! (My children would cringe at the very thought of it!)

CHAPTER FIVE

Take my voice, and let me sing

Always, only, for my King

❋ ❋ ❋

Some of my favourite music has to be black gospel music. It has a rhythm and energy and harmony which are unique.

It was born out of the suffering of black slaves who were imported from Africa into America in the middle of the nineteenth century. They created many of their original songs, known as Negro spirituals, to help them through the day and to encourage one another. They were also used as a way of communicating news and warnings to one another between plantations.

Their hope in their future was undiminished by suffering and their legacy has provided us with a wonderful example of how spiritual music can lift the soul.

NOBODY KNOWS
THE TROUBLE I'VE SEEN

Nobody knows
The trouble I've seen.
Nobody knows but Jesus.
Nobody knows
The trouble I've seen.
Glory Hallelujah!

Sometimes I'm up
Sometimes I'm down
Oh, yes, Lord.
Sometimes I'm almost to the ground
Oh, yes, Lord.

Nobody knows …

I never shall
Forget that day
Oh, yes, Lord,
When Jesus washed my sins away,
Oh, yes, Lord.

Nobody knows …

SWING LOW, SWEET CHARIOT

> *Swing low, sweet chariot,*
> *Comin' for to carry me home!*
> *Swing low, sweet chariot,*
> *Comin' for to carry me home!*

I looked over Jordan and what did I see?
Comin' for to carry me home!
A band of angels comin' after me,
Comin' for to carry me home!

> *Swing low …*

If you get there before I do,
Comin' for to carry me home,
Jus' tell my friends that I'm acomin' too,
Comin' for to carry me home.

> *Swing low …*

I'm sometimes up and sometimes down,
Comin' for to carry me home,
But still my soul feels heavenly bound
Comin' for to carry me home!

> *Swing low …*

STEAL AWAY TO JESUS

Steal away, steal away,
Steal away to Jesus!
Steal away, steal away home,
I ain't got long to stay here.

My Lord calls me;
He calls me by thunder;
The Trumpet sounds within my soul,
I ain't got long to stay here.

Steal away ...

Green trees are bending;
Poor sinner stands atrembling;
The Trumpet sounds within my soul,
I ain't got long to stay here.

Steal away ...

Tombstones are bursting;
Poor sinner stands atrembling;
The Trumpet sounds within my soul,
I ain't got long to stay here.

Steal away ...

The name of Jesus is in my mind as a joyful
song, in my ear as heavenly music and in my
mind, sweet honey.

Richard Rolls, 1290–1349

O for a thousand tongues to sing
My great Redeemer's praise,
The glories of my God and King,
The triumphs of His grace!

Jesus! the name that charms our fears,
That bids our sorrows cease;
'Tis music in the sinner's ears,
'Tis life, and health, and peace.

He speaks, and, listening to His voice,
New life the dead receive,
The mournful, broken hearts rejoice,
The humble poor believe.

Hear Him, ye deaf; His praise, ye dumb,
Your loosened tongues employ:
Ye blind, behold your Saviour come;
And leap, ye lame, for joy.

My gracious Master, and my God,
Assist me to proclaim,
And spread through all the earth abroad,
The honours of Thy name.

Charles Wesley, 1707–88

The soul of one who loves God always swims
in joy, always keeps holiday and is always in a
mood for singing.

St John of the Cross, 1542–91

*S*t Francis of Assisi said, 'Preach the gospel with all
of your life and if necessary, with words.'

I remember someone saying to me once that I had
to earn the right to talk about Jesus. In other words, I
had to let the whole of my life speak of the love of
God, so that people would wonder why!

> And all of us have had that veil removed so
> that we can be mirrors that brightly reflect
> the glory of the Lord. And as the Spirit of
> the Lord works within us, we become more
> and more like him and reflect his glory even
> more.

> *2 Corinthians 3:18, NLT*

> Shout with joy to the LORD, O earth!
> Worship the LORD with gladness.
> Come before him, singing with joy.
> Acknowledge that the LORD is God!
> He made us, and we are his.
> We are his people, the sheep of his pasture.

> Enter his gates with thanksgiving;
> go into his courts with praise.
> Give thanks to him and bless his name.
> For the LORD is good.
> His unfailing love continues for ever,
> and his faithfulness continues to each generation.

> *Psalm 100, NLT*

*P*aul and Silas were praying and singing songs of praise to God after they had been severely beaten and thrown into prison.

Could you?

We 'clothe' ourselves with the character of Jesus, which means changing the way we think and behave. Our character is made up of the sum of our daily habits. Could we make a habit of singing our praise to God in the midst of difficult circumstances?

When I feel the touch
Of Your hand upon my life
It causes me to sing a song
That I love You, Lord.
So from deep within
My spirit singeth unto Thee,
You are my King, You are my God,
And I love you, Lord.

Keri Jones and David Matthew

All our life is a celebration for us: we are convinced, in fact, that God is always everywhere. We sing while we work; sing hymns while we sail; we pray while we carry out all life's other occupations.

Anon.

Alleluya! Sing to Jesus!
His the sceptre, His the throne;
Alleluya! His the triumph
His the victory alone;
Hark! The songs of peaceful Zion
Thunder like a mighty flood;
Jesus, out of every nation,
Hath redeemed us by His blood.

William Chatterton Dix, 1837–98

I sing a simple song of love
To my Saviour, to my Jesus
I'm grateful for the things you've done
My loving Saviour, O precious Jesus
My heart is glad that you've called me your own
There's no place I'd rather be
Than in your arms of love.

Craig Musseau

THE SOLITARY REAPER

Behold her, single in the field,
Yon solitary Highland Lass!
Reaping and singing by herself;
Stop here, or gently pass!
Alone she cuts and binds the grain,
And sings a melancholy strain;
O listen! for the Vale profound
Is overflowing with the sound.

No Nightingale did ever chaunt
So sweetly to reposing bands
Of travellers in some shady haunt,
Among Arabian sands:
No sweeter voice was ever heard
In spring-time from the Cuckoo-bird,
Breaking the silence of the seas
Among the farthest Hebrides.

Will no one tell me what she sings? –
Perhaps the plaintive numbers flow
For old, unhappy, far-off things,
And battles long ago:
Or is it some more humble lay,
Familiar matter of to-day?
Some natural sorrow, loss, or pain,
That has been, and may be again?

Whate'er the theme, the Maiden sang
As if her song could have no ending;
I saw her singing at her work,
And o'er the sickle bending; –
I listened till I had my fill;
And, as I mounted up the hill,
The music in my heart I bore,
Long after it was heard no more.

William Wordsworth, 1770–1850

*B*efore I met my husband he made an album which included the following song. Although the sentiments are now rather quaint and old-fashioned, I think Roy really believed and lived the words he sang.

If I can help somebody as I pass along
If I can cheer somebody with a word or a song
If I can show somebody he is travelling wrong,
Then my living shall not be in vain.

If I can do my duty as a good man ought
If I can bring back beauty to a world of rot
If I can spread love's message that the Master
    taught
Then my living shall not be in vain.

Alma Bazel Androzzo

MY JESUS, MY SAVIOUR

My Jesus, my Saviour,
Lord, there is none like You.
All of my days I want to praise
the wonders of Your mighty love.
My comfort, my shelter,
tower of refuge and strength,
let every breath, all that I am,
never cease to worship You.

Shout to the Lord all the earth, let us sing
power and majesty, praise to the King.
Mountains bow down and the seas will
      roar
at the sound of Your name.
I sing for joy at the work of Your hands,
for ever I'll love You, for ever I'll stand.
Nothing compares to the promise I have
      in you.

    My Jesus, my Saviour ...

      Darlene Zschech

Questions to ponder

❊ ❊ ❊

1 Francis of Assisi's challenge was that we should preach
   the gospel through the way we live our lives. If people
   had to give a description of Christianity through what
   they see in you, what would they say?

2 Do you take the time to build friendships with people in
   order to 'earn the right' to tell them about Jesus?

3 Compose your own psalm as a love song to Jesus.

June

❀ ❀ ❀

There's an old saying, 'In June, the cuckoo changes his tune', and it's true, isn't it? I love to listen out for the first cuckoo singing in spring, knowing that by June I will have missed him – it's too late! His voice will blend in with the myriad birdsongs, no longer distinctive.

> He was but as the cuckoo is in June,
> Heard, not regarded.
>
> *William Shakespeare, 1564–1616*

Sometimes we feel heard, but not regarded. We are insignificant, blending in with the rest of the world, going its way. Sometimes we feel we have no voice but we want to shout about injustices to our fellow human beings.

But we do have a voice and we can use it on behalf of the voiceless.

Never underestimate the difference one voice can make, when raised on behalf of another – to encourage, rebuke, support, challenge and help. One letter of approval, praise or criticism sent to a radio or TV station is estimated to represent one thousand people who might have similar views.

Think of the influence we could have if we took the trouble to applaud all the good programmes. Think of the influence we could have if we all took the trouble to lobby against human rights injustices.

This month ask God to enable you to speak out for him on behalf of the persecuted, voiceless people in our world.

CHAPTER SIX

Take my lips, and let them be

Filled with messages from Thee

❊ ❊ ❊

I heard a story of a woman who complained loudly to an airline stewardess that she did not want to sit next to the person beside her because he was of a different race. She insisted on being moved and refused to take no for an answer when told that the plane was full. Eventually the stewardess said she would ask the captain if there were any seats available in business or first class. A few minutes later she returned and said, 'There is a seat available in first class. Would you care to gather your belongings and come with me, sir!'

A round of applause followed from the other passengers!

> People may forget what you said
> People may forget what you did
> But people will never forget how
> you made them feel.

Anon.

God loves and Jesus died for the person you like least in the whole world.

Most of us are not aware how deeply rooted our prejudices are until we are confronted with them. We think of prejudices as racial, cultural, political or religious, but how about the way we like things done? Because we've 'always done it like that', we believe we must be right – but because others do the same things differently, are they wrong?

Very often, our prejudices are based on fear, because of lack of security and understanding. So we build barriers of suspicion and hostility and become defensive instead of holding out the hand of friendship and love, building bridges which will enable us to see others as equally loved by God.

> Beauty for brokenness, hope for despair,
> Lord, in Your suffering world this is our
> prayer.
> Bread for the children, justice, joy, peace,
> Sunrise to sunset, Your kingdom increase!
>
> Shelter for fragile lives, cures for their ills
> Work for the craftsmen, trade for their
> skills;
> Land for the dispossessed, rights for the
> weak,
> Voices to plead their cause of those who
> can't speak.

God of the poor, friend of the weak,
Give us compassion we pray:
Melt our cold hearts,
Let tears fall like rain;
Come, change our love
From a spark to a flame.

Refuge from cruel wars, havens from fear,
Cities for sanctuary, freedoms to share.
Peace to the killing-fields, scorched earth to
    green,
Christ for the bitterness, His cross for the
    pain.

Rest for the ravaged earth, oceans and streams
Plundered and poisoned – our future, our
    dreams.
Lord, end our madness, carelessness, greed;
Make us content with the things that we need.

God of the poor ...

Lighten our darkness, breathe on this flame
Until Your justice burns brightly again;
Until the nations learn of Your ways
Seek Your salvation and bring You their praise.

God of the poor ...

Graham Kendrick

I have a dream that one day every valley shall be exalted, every hill and mountain shall be made low, the rough places will be made plains, and the crooked places will be made straight, and the glory of the Lord shall be revealed, and all flesh shall see it together.

Isaiah 40:4

Each time a man stands up for an idea, or acts to improve the lot of others, or strikes out against injustice, he sends forth a tiny ripple of hope, and crossing each other from a million different centres of energy and daring, those ripples build a current that can sweep down the mightiest walls of oppression and resistance.

Few are willing to brave the disapproval of their fellows, the censure of their colleagues, the wrath of their society. Moral courage is a rarer commodity than bravery in battle or greater intelligence. Yet it is the one essential, vital quality for those who seek to change a world that yields most painfully to change.

Robert Kennedy, 1925–68

Lord I stand in the midst of a multitude
Of those from every tribe and tongue
We are your people redeemed by your blood
Rescued from death by your love
There are no words good enough to thank you
There are no words to express my praise
But I will lift up my voice and sing from my
       heart
With all of my strength

Hallelujah, Hallelujah, Hallelujah to the lamb
Hallelujah, Hallelujah by the blood of Christ we
       stand
Every tongue, every tribe, every people, every land
Giving glory, giving honour, giving praise
Unto the Lamb of God.

Lord we stand by grace in your presence
Cleansed by the blood of the Lamb
We are your children called by your name
Humbly we bow and we pray
Release your power to work in us and through
       us
Till we are changed to be more like you
Then all the nations will see your glory revealed
And worship you

Hallelujah, Hallelujah ...

       Don Moen and Debbye Graafsma

Do not do anything you hate to another.
You do not like it when someone slanders
you? Then do not slander anyone. You do
not like it if someone denounces you falsely?
Then do not denounce anyone. You do not
like it if someone despises you, injures you,
or steals something from you? Then do
nothing of this sort to another. He who can
keep this saying has what he needs for
salvation.

Fourth-century saying

Many people find fault as if there were a
reward in it.

Anon.

Kind words can be short and easy to speak
but their echoes are truly endless.

Mother Teresa of Calcutta, 1910–97

No one needs kindness more than someone
who doesn't deserve it.

Anon.

*If you were paid ten pence for every kind word you
ever spoke and had to pay out five pence for every
unkind word, would you be rich or poor?*

Keep your words soft and sweet just in case
you have to eat them.

Anon.

Don't speak evil against each other, my dear
brothers and sisters.

James 4:11, NLT

If aught good thou canst not say
Of thy brother, foe or friend,
Take thou then the silent way
Lest in word thou should'st offend.

Anon.

The one who is absent should be safe among
those who are present.

Anon.

We should have great peace if we did not
busy ourselves with what others say and do.

Thomas à Kempis, 1380–1471

Those who can control their tongues can also control themselves in every other way.

James 3:2, NLT

What! Never speak one evil word,
Or rash, or idle, or unkind!
Oh, how shall I, most gracious Lord,
This mark of true perfection find?

Charles Wesley, 1707–88

Nothing is opened in error more than the mouth.

Anon.

Men of few words are the best men.

William Shakespeare, 1564–1616

We declare Your majesty
We proclaim that Your name is exalted
For You reign magnificently, rule victoriously
And Your power is shown throughout the
      earth.

And we exclaim, 'Our God is mighty!'
Lift up Your name for You are holy.
Sing it again, all honour and glory –
In adoration we bow before Your throne!

Malcolm du Plessis

*D*uring the nineteenth century, D. L. Moody once heard someone say, 'The world has yet to see what God can do with one man who is completely yielded to him.' Moody's response was, 'By God's grace, I'll be that man.' He became one of the greatest evangelists the world had known to that time.

You can't go on heavenly missions without heavenly fire.

D. L. Moody, 1837–99

God sends no one away empty except those who are full of themselves.

D. L. Moody, 1837–99

Tell out, my soul, the greatness of the
    Lord!
Unnumbered blessings, give my spirit voice;
tender to me the promise of his word;
in God my Saviour shall my heart rejoice.

Tell out, my soul, the greatness of his
    Name!
Make known his might, the deeds his arm
    has done;
his mercy sure, from age to age the same;
his holy Name, the Lord, the Mighty One.

Tell out, my soul, the greatness of his
    might!
Powers and dominions lay their glory by.
Proud hearts and stubborn wills are put to
    flight,
the hungry fed, the humble lifted high.

Tell out, my soul, the glories of his word!
Firm is his promise, and his mercy sure.
Tell out, my soul, the greatness of the Lord
to children's children and for evermore!

Timothy Dudley-Smith

Jesus came and told his disciples, 'I have been given complete authority in heaven and on earth. Therefore, go and make disciples of all the nations, baptising them in the name of the Father and the Son and the Holy Spirit. Teach these new disciples to obey all the commands I have given you. And be sure of this: I am with you always, even to the end of the age.'

Matthew 28:18–20, NLT

*T*hese were the last words of Jesus in Matthew's Gospel, and they are words that every Christian takes very seriously. They are the words which call missionaries to go to all the nations to share the love of Jesus and his saving power.

And how can they believe in him if they have never heard about him? And how can they hear about him unless someone tells them?

Romans 10:14, NLT

*F*rom the moment Jesus came into my life I was so excited I wanted to share what had happened with everyone I met! I knew other people's lives could be different too, if only they knew about him. That desire has never gone away, even after more than quarter of a century. I love to be able to tell people that Jesus changes us from the inside. Rules and regulations and resolutions are only a determination to change on the outside, which is why, unless we have enormous will power, they won't last for very long!

The world outside may never come to church to hear a sermon, but the outside world sees us every day and our lives must be the sermon to them of new life.

William Barclay, 1907–78

We hear your call to 'Go' –
'Go and make disciples', identify with
        strangers, walk on shifting sands and
        build a kingdom church.
'Go' is not a comfortable word.
Teach us how to depend on you again:
we need your initiative, your boldness, your
        blessing, your plan.
Make us unafraid to break new ground,
to take new faith steps with you.

Do a new thing, Father, in your Army.
Give a new passion for worship, a new love
    for the lost,
a new unity in purpose, and a new strength
    in our resolve,
a new heart of repentance, a new humanity
    of spirit,
a new pulse for the people, a new heart laid
    bare.

And send us out.

A Salvation Army prayer

If you tell the truth, you don't have to remember anything.

Mark Twain, 1835–1910

Today, if ye will hear his voice,
Harden not your heart.

Psalm 95:7–8, AV

He that has promised pardon on our repentance has not promised to preserve our lives until we repent.

Francis Quarles, 1592–1644

You cannot repent too soon, because you do not know how soon it will be too late.

Thomas Fuller, 1608–61

Thousands of people are happy without God in this world. If I was happy and moral till Jesus came, why did He come? Because that kind of happiness and peace is on a wrong level; Jesus Christ came to send a sword through every peace that is not based on a personal relationship to Himself.

Oswald Chambers, 1874–1917

Many people who plan to meet God at the eleventh hour die at 10.30.

Anon.

Consider the lilies of the field, how they grow, they simply are! Think of the sea, the air, the sun, the stars and the moon – all these are, and what a ministration they exert. So often we mar God's designed influence through *us* by our self-conscious effort to be consistent and useful. Jesus says that there is only one way to develop spiritually and that is by concentration on God. 'Do not bother

about being of use to others, believe on Me'
– pay attention to the *Source*, and out of you
will flow rivers of living water. We cannot
get at the springs of our natural life by
common sense, and Jesus is teaching that
growth in spiritual life does not depend on
our *watching* it, but on concentration on our
Father in heaven. Our heavenly Father *knows*
the circumstances we are in, and if we *keep*
concentrated on Him *we* will grow spiritually
as the lilies.

The people who influence us most are not
those who buttonhole us and talk to us, but
those who live their lives like the stars in
heaven and the lilies of the field, perfectly
simply and unaffectedly. Those are the lives
that mould us.

If you want to be of *use* to God, get
rightly related to Jesus Christ and He will
make you of *use* unconsciously every minute
you live.

Oswald Chambers, 1874–1917

And our lives? We talk of inviting God into
our lives. No, God invites us into his
worldview.

We ask where God fits in our life-story.
God asks where our lives fit into his story.

We want to apply the Bible to our lives.
God asks us to apply our lives to the Bible.

We wonder what kind of mission God has for me. The question is what kind of me God wants for his mission.

We wonder how to make the Gospel relevant to the world. God's agenda is transforming the world to the shape of the Gospel.

I've got Jesus deep down in my heart? Yes, but far greater is that my life is hid with Christ in God.

Chris Wright, LICC magazine

Your real life is hidden with Christ in God.

Colossians 3:3, NLT

Just let me say how much I love you
Let me speak of your mercy and grace
Just let me live in the shadow of your
      beauty
Let me see you face to face
And the earth will shake as your word goes
      forth
And the heavens can tremble and fall
Just let me say how much I love you
O my Saviour and my friend.

Just let me hear your finest whispers
As you gently call my name.
And let me see your power and your glory
Let me feel your Spirit's flame,
Let me find you in the desert,
'til this sand is holy ground,
and I am found completely surrendered
to you my Lord and friend.

So let me say how much I love you,
With all my heart I long for you.
For I am caught in this passion of knowing
This endless love I've found in you.
And the depth of grace, the forgiveness
     found
To be called a child of God,
Just makes me say how much I love you
My Saviour, my Lord and friend.

Geoff Bullock

Questions to ponder

❋ ❋ ❋

1 You have 'a voice'. How could you use it to stand up against injustice, or to make life better for even one person?

2 How can you support Fair Trade? Find out more about sweatshop labour, etc.

3 Pray for those who are being persecuted and thank God that he supplies all our needs (not necessarily our wants).

4 Contact Jubilee Action, Christian Solidarity Worldwide and Open Doors, to find out how to become involved with writing letters to ambassadors, MPs, political prisoners, etc.

July

July is the month when many people will be preparing to go on holiday. Exams are over, schools close for the long break. In theory the hazy, lazy days of summer stretch ahead, suggesting relaxation and luxurious treats and adventures.

But for others the expectation will be very different – no comfortable beach loungers at the poolside of a five-star hotel – no thoughts of planning a holiday for them. This can give rise to envy and the temptation to get into debt by taking out loans in order to bolster self-esteem.

It's not what we have but how we use what we have that matters to God. During these sunshine weeks, take time out to sort out priorities.

Think of what you spend needlessly, which could be saved or used more wisely. For instance, the price of a cappuccino each day while waiting to catch the train to work could sponsor a child in Uganda to be fed and educated. Who knows what such an investment might do for that child and what they might be able to achieve as a result of your generosity?

CHAPTER SEVEN

Take my silver and my gold

Not a mite would I withhold

* * *

*P*eople seem to think that money is the answer to all problems and will meet their deepest needs. Why, otherwise, would there be lotteries, scratch cards and TV quiz programmes such as Who Wants to be a Millionaire?

So many people ruin their lives by overspending, using credit cards, taking out loans, thus getting into debt that can take a lifetime to clear. They imagine that if only they had enough money, everything would be all right and problems would disappear.

John D. Rockefeller, one of the world's wealthiest men, was asked how much money he would need to be satisfied. His reply? 'Just a little more.'

Wealth is relative. I remember as a teenager saving up for months for a sweater I had seen in a shop window, until I could afford to buy it! There were no credit cards in those days and it wouldn't have occurred to me to borrow. I had to wait till, coins in hand, I could make that sensational transaction!

Why spend your money on food that does
not give you strength? Why pay for food that
does you no good? Listen, and I will tell you
where to get food that is good for the soul!

Isaiah 55:2, NLT

We spend money we can't afford, to buy things
we don't use, to impress people we don't like.
Have you noticed that a few weeks after you have
made the purchase, the excitement has worn off and
you're on to the next thing? Nothing satisfies for very
long. It can control your whole life as you strive for
bigger, better, more powerful and more luxurious
items.

The *love* of money is at the root of all kinds
of evil. And some people, craving money,
have wandered from the faith and pierced
themselves with many sorrows.

1 Timothy 6:10, NLT

Money can do absolutely everything that doesn't matter.

He who has money to spare, has it always in his power to benefit others; and of such power a good man must always be desirous.

Samuel Johnson, 1709–86

God loves a cheerful giver.

2 Corinthians 9:7, NIV

Money itself is a neutral method of exchange. The way we handle it definitely is not. It can represent power, status, corruption and control. It can also represent poverty, starvation and deprivation, injustice and envy. The Bible teaches that it is ours to be used to glorify God – not to become a god in itself.

Spending money is easy. Everything else you do with it is difficult.

Anon.

Trust in your money and down you go!

Proverbs 11:28, NLT

We know what it is to lose health, wealth and reputation ... But what is the loss of all those things compared with the loss of the soul?

D. L. Moody, 1837–99

If you try to keep your life for yourself, you will lose it. But if you give up your life for my sake and for the sake of the Good News, you will find true life.

Mark 8:35, NLT

Too often we spend our time spending money as an escape, or to fill an emptiness in our lives. If we pursue money as an ambition and goal, we might live in comfort, but spiritually become poor.

We are merely moving shadows,
and all our busy rushing ends in nothing.
We heap up wealth for someone else to spend.
And so, Lord, where do I put my hope?
My only hope is in you.

Psalm 39:6–7, NLT

People, for the sake of getting a living, forget to live.

Everything we have has come from you and we give you only what you have already given us.

1 Chronicles 29:16

Give fools their gold and know their power.
Let fortune's bubbles rise and fall.
Who sows a field or trains a flower,
Or plants a tree – is more than all.

Anon.

Give to him that asketh thee. 'Why do we always make this mean money?' Our Lord makes no mention of money. The blood of most of us seems to run in gold. The reason we make it mean money is because that is where our heart is.

Oswald Chambers, 1874–1917

A contented person is the one who enjoys the scenery on a detour.

Anon.

In all the developing countries I have been to, I have been horrifyingly aware of the difference between their lifestyles and mine in terms of comfort and expectation. After my first experience of this, I came home determined to clear out the clutter of my life. I have so much that I store up, so much that I never use but might come in useful and so much that takes up my time and attention, which could be used more productively. For what I noticed was not only their poverty but their wealth. They cared about each other (because they had few 'things'). They shared what they had and they were content with themselves. How much have we in the West lost, because of our accumulation of material 'things'?

We get a living by what we get.
We get a life by what we give.

Anon.

It is loss to keep when God says, 'Give'.

Anon.

Those who shut their ears to the cries of the poor will be ignored in their own time of need.

Proverbs 21:13, NLT

SEEN ON A WAYSIDE PULPIT

Money will buy a bed but not sleep;
food but not appetite;
finery but not beauty;
a house but not a home;
luxuries but not culture;
amusement but not happiness;
religion but not salvation;
a passport to everywhere – but heaven.

Why don't people think about what they
have instead of what they haven't?

Roy Castle

For I have learned to get along happily
whether I have much or little. I know how
to live on almost nothing or with everything.
I have learned the secret of living in every
situation.

Paul to the Philippians (Phil. 4:11–12, NLT)

God has given gifts to each of you ...
Manage them well so that God's generosity
can flow through you.

1 Peter 4:10, NLT

When you have eaten your fill, praise the
Lord your God for the good land he has
given you. But that is the time to be careful!
Beware that in your plenty you do not forget
the Lord your God and disobey his
commands, regulations, and laws ... Do not
become proud at that time and forget the
Lord your God.

Deuteronomy 8:10–14, NLT

How many times have you heard someone say
'If I had his money I could do things my way'?
But little they know, it's so hard to find
One rich man in ten with a satisfied mind.

Once I was living in fortune and fame.
Everything that I dreamed of to get a start in
life's game.
Then suddenly it happened. I lost every dime.
But I'm richer by far with a satisfied mind.

'Cause money can't buy back your youth
      when you're old
or a friend when you're lonely
or love that's grown cold.
The wealthiest person is a pauper at times
Compared to the man with a satisfied mind.

When life has ended my time has run out
My friends and my loved ones I'll leave there's
      no doubt
But one thing for certain when it comes to my
      time
I'll leave this old world with a satisfied mind.

Red Hayes and Jack Rhodes

Those who lose money, lose much
Those who lose a friend, lose more
Those who lose faith, lose all.

Anon.

Our true riches lie, not in the acceptance or rejection of the material as though nothing else existed, but in our ready acceptance of the spiritual, and in the possession of a continuing experience of the presence and power of the Holy Spirit. Rich, not in the ephemera of the supermarket, but in those things 'which the world cannot give' – love, joy and peace.

Lord, I'm rich.
I'm rich because you love me, and I
     know it.
Rich beyond anything the world can give.
Rich because the world can't take it away.
It's there, your love, and nothing I do will
     change it.
I can reject it, forget it,
but it's still there.
I only have to reach out and it's mine.

I'm rich because of faith. Because, knowing
     your love, I can believe the rest.
When I'm down, things get unreal.
Disconnected.
It's so easy to question,
to hang my insecurity on to you.
To blame you for my own weakness,
to say there's something wrong with the
     system
when I know it's me.
And then your love takes over again,
and the joy bursts out.
Like living grass through dead concrete.

I'm rich because of hope.
Because your love gives me a new
        perspective on life.
I may get tired and disappointed.
Things go wrong,
and I wonder what it's all about.
Then I reach out and feel that love again.
And I know that beyond the
        disappointment,
beyond the cares, you are there.
Always.
And my hope is real, it can't be taken
        away.
I may give it up, but it can't be taken
        away.
Yes, Lord, I'm rich,
and it has nothing to do with
        supermarkets.
It's not baked beans,
or this week's special offer, it's you.
You, Lord, your love, and joy, and peace.

Eddie Askew

Treasure in Heaven is faith that has been tried.

Oswald Chambers, 1874–1917

Questions to ponder

❋ ❋ ❋

1 *Is money your God?*

2 *It has been said that whatever gets your attention gets you! Does your attention to money get you?*

3 *Are you satisfied with what you have or are you always wanting more? Are you in need?*

4 *'If you need something, give something away.' Are you prepared to give everything you own to God and let him govern what happens to it?*

August

***

Traditionally August is the time when many people are relaxing from their normal chores and activities.

My husband was brought up in a small Yorkshire village where most of the inhabitants worked in the local woollen mill. For two weeks the mill would close down and coachloads of its workers would make for the coast – in many cases to Blackpool. This was a blissful break from the monotony and routine of the milling process – a chance to see life in a different dimension, to meet new people and to play!

God gave us the Sabbath for rest. He knew that the human mind and body needed rest and refreshment and He set us His example of drawing aside and reflecting.

An old saying I remember from my childhood is true: 'All work and no play makes Jack a dull boy!' Not all of us can manage to get away for a holiday, but this month if you can, change your routine; determine to leave the chores, take time to walk, to read, to meet up with some friends, go to the theatre and have some fun!

What is this life if, full of care,
We have no time to stand and stare.

W. H. Davies, 1871–1940

CHAPTER EIGHT

Take my intellect, and use

Every power as Thou shalt choose

❋ ❋ ❋

A man is known for the company his mind keeps.

Anon.

The well-known story about a drowning man is a good illustration of the fact that although God calls us to trust him in everything, he also credits us with a brain and common sense!

After exceptionally heavy rainfall a man discovered that the ground floor of his house was flooded, so he went upstairs to wait for the floods to subside. While he was watching, a boat went by the window and the boatman offered to row him to safety. 'No, I'm trusting the Lord to save me,' he replied.

However, the continuing rain forced him to climb out of the window and onto the roof. At that moment a low-flying helicopter hovered overhead and a man shouted down that he would throw him a safety harness and haul him into the helicopter. 'It's all right,' said the man. 'I'm trusting the Lord to save me.' Eventually an enormous wave swept him off the roof and he drowned.

When he got to heaven, he questioned God. 'I was trusting you – why didn't you save me?'

'Well,' God replied, 'I sent you a boat and a helicopter.'

We all make choices every day of our lives – when to get up, what to wear, what to eat. We make them without even thinking about them. But we always face the consequences of those choices – too much, too little, too late.

We also face life-changing choices: where to live, what job to take, who to marry, how to behave, and we live with the consequences of those choices, right or wrong.

That is why it is so important to ask God to help us with those choices and make the right decisions. How? Through prayer.

> Jesus Christ lived in the moral domain and in a sense, the intellect is no use there. Intellect is not a guide, but an instrument.
>
> *Anon.*

> Prayer is the international ballistic missile that hits the target every time.
>
> *Jim Graham*

Prayer is not getting God into my world to meet my needs, but getting me into his world to serve his purposes.

Jim Graham

May the mind of Christ my Saviour
Live in me from day to day,
By his love and power controlling
All I do and say.

May the word of God dwell richly
In my heart from hour to hour,
So that all may see I triumph
Only through His power.

May the peace of God my Father
Rule my life in everything,
That I may be calm to comfort
Sick and sorrowing.

May the love of Jesus fill me,
As the waters fill the sea;
Him exalting, self abasing,
This is victory.

May I run the race before me,
Strong and brave to face the foe,
Looking only unto Jesus,
As I onward go.

Kate Barclay Wilkinson, 1859–1928

The LORD says, 'I will guide you along the
best pathway for your life. I will advise you
and watch over you.'

Psalm 32:8, NLT

*T*his was one of the first verses I read after becoming
a Christian and it was miraculous to think God
had mapped out a path for my life and as long as I was
prepared to allow him to guide me, his peace would
remain with me, however mountainous or obstacle-
filled the pathway might be. But then God grabbed my
attention in a different way through this verse.

One of my many fears as I coped with my children
was that of keeping control. The responsibility for
those precious lives weighed heavily upon me and I
had to make sure I held the reins very tightly. I had
been brought up under very strict discipline (which I
have never regretted) and I saw this as a vital part of
my role as a mother. If I ever let go of those reins I
thought I would fall apart and so would the family.

God began to challenge me about the way I was
handling my children. He began gently to prise my
fingers so tightly wrapped about those reins. If God
had a plan for my life, then surely he had a plan for
the life of each of my children. Because we are all
unique, those plans would all be different. I had
begun to trust God with every aspect of my life and
my future. I had to trust him with my children's. As I
put this principle into practice, I sensed, once again,
amazing freedom and release.

Like all caring parents, I wanted the best for my children. The way I had been putting it into practice was not very wise. It also caused a good deal of stress. God's ways are not always our ways – His wisdom is far greater.

As a result of this revelation, my prayer for them became, not that they would be brightest and best and top and most, but that they would discover for themselves the plans God had for their lives.

'My thoughts are completely different from yours' says the LORD. 'And my ways are far beyond anything you could imagine. For just as the heavens are higher than the earth, so are my ways higher than your ways and my thoughts higher than your thoughts.'

Isaiah 55:8–9, NLT

There is another kind of silence to be cultivated, besides that of the tongue as regards others. I mean silence as regards one's self – restraining the imagination, not permitting it to dwell overmuch on what we have heard or said, not indulging in the phantasmagoria of picture-thoughts, whether of the past or future. Be sure that you have made no small progress in the spiritual life, when you can control your imagination, so as to fix it on the duty and occupation actually existing, to the exclusion of the crowd of thoughts which are perpetually sweeping across the mind. No doubt, you cannot prevent those thoughts from arising, but you can prevent yourself from dwelling on them; you can put them aside, you can check the self-complacency, or irritation, or earthly longings which feed them, and by the practice of such control of your thoughts you will attain that spirit of inward silence which draws the soul into a close intercourse with God.

Jean N. Grou

You do not get rid of a temptation
    by yielding to it.
Temptation is a thought.
Yielded to, it becomes an act.
An act becomes a habit.
A habit becomes a lifestyle.

Anon.

Just as pain is God's warning that something is wrong with our body, so conscience is God's warning that something is wrong with our behaviour.

Nothing doth so much establish the mind amidst the rollings and turbulency of present things, as both a look above them, and a look beyond them; above them to the good and steady Hand by which they are ruled, and beyond them to the sweet and beautiful end to which, by that Hand, they shall be brought ... Study pure and holy walking, if you would have your confidence firm, and have boldness and joy in God. You will find that a little sin will shake your trust and disturb your peace more than the greatest sufferings: yea, in those sufferings, your assurance and joy in God will grow and abound most if sin be kept out. So much sin as gets in, so much peace will go out.

R. Leighton, 1611–84

There's something here for each one of us. I've known people in depression: full of remorse and guilt, unable to see light or hope, seeing only their own unworthiness. I've known others, just unable to believe that Christ's love is for them, because they don't merit it. All right, none of us is worthy, but that's not the criterion. Love isn't created by the 'niceness' or worthiness of our natures. The truth is, thank God, that love springs from the nature of the one who loves, that is, from God. It is because God is love that we are loved and '... this is for us the perfection of love, to have confidence on the day of judgement, and this we can have ...' (1 John 4:17, NEB). Read the rest for yourself.

And that love, incarnate in Jesus, brought forgiveness for all who will take it – Judas, or me – and that is our confidence, our hope,

our certainty. If only … Judas had waited …
what a witness he would have made! Think
of Paul, the killer of Christians, the enemy of
Christ, and yet later exulting 'Christ lives in
me'. I wonder what the Gospel according to
Judas could have been? Perhaps it would
have begun, 'Hold onto hope, love is alive,
strong, and flowering anew above the dark
earth. Hallelujah.'

Eddie Askew

The dividing line between good and evil
runs through every human heart.

Aleksandr Solzhenitsyn

'*T*here is no such thing as absolute truth.'
Is that true?!

If a million people do the wrong thing, that
still doesn't make it right.

Anon.

The key to greatness is to be in reality what we appear to be.

Socrates, 469–399 BC

Integrity is a commitment to do what is right, regardless of the cost ... it is being governed by settled convictions instead of momentary expediency ... by principles rather than pragmatism ... by vision rather than comfort ... by mission rather than politics ... by God's will rather than human whim ... for God's kingdom rather than our own.

Anon.

When integrity is in control your words and your heart will be in agreement.

Anon.

Speak when you're angry and you'll make the best speech you'll ever regret!

Our first task in approaching another person is to take off our shoes – for the place we are approaching is holy ground. Otherwise we may find ourselves treading on another's dream. More serious still we may forget that God was there before our arrival.

Mrs Charles E. Cowman, Fear Not

Stormy wind, fulfilling His word.

Psalm 148:8, NASB

Stormy winds come not without mercy and blessing. There is music in the blast if we listen aright. Is there no music in the heart of sorrow that the Lord of all has chosen for His own? Are you not nearer to the Master, have you not grown in faith, in patience, in prayerfulness, in thankful hope, since the time the storm winds first sighed across your life?

Do not tremble because of the winds of the future; your Lord will be living and loving tomorrow, even as He lives and loves today, and no storm waits in your path but shall leave behind another record that your Heavenly Father is stronger than the tempest, nearer than the grief.

We are travelling home to that beauteous shore where the chill winds never sweep, the hurricane makes no moan; yet, amid the rest of the painless Homeland, shall we not love the Lord a thousandfold more for every storm of earth in which He drew near to us, saying, 'Fear not,' and held us by the hand, and tenderly bore us through the hour that seemed the darkest? We shall glorify Him then that He has been to us, again and again, a cover from the blast; but let us not wait to glorify Him till the blast is over.

Even now let us give thanks that all the winds of life – the rough ones as well as those that blow from the south – are of His appointing.

Set your thoughts, not on the storm, but on the Love that rules the storm; then the winds of trouble shall no longer seem as sad and restless voices, but as an Aeolian harp attuned to peace, to hope, to everlasting victory.

Occupy your minds with good thoughts, or the enemy will fill them with bad ones; unoccupied they cannot be.

Thomas More, 1478–1535

Fix your thoughts on what is true and honourable and right. Think about things that are pure and lovely and admirable. Think about things that are excellent and worthy of praise.

Philippians 4:8, NLT

YOU ARE PRECIOUS

As a teacher teaches best by sparking curiosity, so a friend encourages best by kindling self-worth.

Recently a dear friend was talking with me about her struggle to realise her own worth.

'The other day,' she said, 'I was so frustrated with my slow progress, wondering if I would ever really learn to be kind to myself. Then I thought of you and another friend who have affirmed me for so many years, believing in me even when I didn't honour my own opinions and feelings, and making me feel special when I didn't place much value on myself. And I suddenly understood something that's helping me be more patient with myself.

'I realised that you've loved me a lot longer than I've loved myself, so you're better at it! I know where that kind of love comes from. And I know that in time, I'll get better at it too.'

What a privilege God has given us to love one another! When the apostle Paul instructed us to observe whatever is true, noble, right, pure, lovely, admirable, excellent and praiseworthy (Phil. 4:8), he handed us a delightful set of tools to carve self-worth into the lives of others. As we see and affirm these positive qualities in our friends, our friends begin to see the Source of all that is true and excellent and praiseworthy. And soon they begin praising their lovely Creator by becoming all he meant for them to be.

Susan L. Lenzkes

But now, this is what the Lord says – he who created you … he who formed you … 'Fear not, for I have redeemed you; I have summoned you by name, you are mine … You are precious and honoured in my sight … I love you … Forget the former things; do not dwell on the past. See, I am doing a new thing! Now it springs up; do you not perceive it?

Isaiah 43:1–4, 18–19

And I pray that Christ will be more and more at home in your hearts as you trust in him. May your roots go down deep into the soil of God's marvellous love. And may you have the power to understand, as all God's people should, how wide, how long, how high, and how deep his love really is.

Ephesians 3:17–18, NLT

Through all the changing scenes of life,
In trouble and in joy,
The praises of my God shall still
My heart and tongue employ.

O magnify the Lord with me,
With me exalt His name;
When in distress to Him I called,
He to my rescue came.

The hosts of God encamp around
The dwellings of the just;
Deliverance He affords to all
Who on His succour trust.

O make but trial of His love;
Experience will decide
How blest they are, and only they,
Who in His truth confide.

To Father, Son and Holy Ghost
The God whom we adore
Be glory as it was, is now
And shall be evermore.

Nahum Tate, 1652–1715, and
Nicholas Brady, 1639–1726

*P*aul tells the Philippians:

Fix your thoughts on what is true and
honourable and right.

D*o you?*

Think about things that are pure and lovely and admirable.

D*o you?*

Think about things that are excellent and worthy of praise.

D*o you?*

Keep putting into practice all you learned from me and heard from me and saw me doing.

D*o you? To do that, it is necessary to read and apply Paul's teaching to the Philippians. Then:*

'The God of peace will be with you.'

Questions to ponder

❋ ❋ ❋

1 What are you feeding your mind with these days?

2 What is going on in your life that you wouldn't want anyone else to know about? If you nurture a thought for long enough, it will become a behaviour and whatever behaviour or thought you tolerate, you will never change.

3 Start monitoring your mindset and work on your attitude, your prejudices, your temptations and thought patterns, until you, with the hymn writer, can ask the Lord to use your intellect in whatever way he chooses.

September

*A*lthough this month leads us into autumn, it is also a time of new beginnings for many – new schools, new classes, new colleges and universities, new friends. Sometimes taking a step into the unknown can be scary! We tend to like the security of routine and we certainly don't want change which might cause us pain or suffering.

Yet if we choose God's way, we have to be prepared to face whatever life throws at us. In order to grow, in order to learn, we have to take risks and step out into the unknown.

The credit belongs to the man who is actually in the arena, whose face is marred in the dust and sweat and blood; who spends himself in a worthy cause, who, at best, knows the triumph of high achievement and who, at the worst, if he fails, at least fails while daring greatly, so that his face shall never be with those cold and timid souls who know neither victory nor defeat.

Theodore Roosevelt, 1858–1919

Which kind of person are you intending to be?

CHAPTER NINE

Take my will, and make it Thine

It shall be no longer mine

✻ ✻ ✻

*J*esus said in the Garden of Gethsemane, the night before he was crucified, 'My father! If it is possible, let this cup of suffering be taken away from me. Yet I want your will, not mine.'

Even Jesus, with all the power of the Son of God, found the pain of his suffering almost too hard to bear. But, knowing his purpose, he was willing to submit to his Father's will.

Many of us have gone through sufferings we would have longed to sidestep; hoping we would wake up from a bad dream. But life's not like that and the reality of pain, suffering and grief is very acute. We paraphrase those words of Jesus in our moment of desolation. 'Lord, I don't want to go through this terrible experience, but if it's part of your purpose for my life, it's all right.'

When I became a Christian, I learnt that it's not so much what happens to me that's important, it's how I handle what happens.

Problems are growth activators. We learn more in the tough times than we do when life is easy.

161

So if you are suffering according to God's will, keep on doing what is right, and trust yourself to the God who made you, for he will never fail you.

1 Peter 4:19, NLT

To choose to suffer means there is something wrong; to choose God's will even if it means suffering is a very different thing. No healthy person would choose to suffer. He or she chooses God's will, as Jesus did, whether it involves suffering or not.

As a mother, I would have protected my children from any kind of danger, sickness, suffering or pain. That protective instinct never goes away, even when the children are adults. When they were babies, and found it difficult to breathe when they had a chest cold, I wished I could have taken it from them because I knew how to cope. But I also understood this was not possible and that every illness helped to build up their immune system. When they were growing up and went through disappointments, broken relationships, I would have gladly taken that pain from them, but I couldn't and besides, those experiences help them to realise that life isn't always easy and doesn't always turn out the way we hope or expect. Then I could only encourage them to know that the Lord knew and cared and so did I!

Much that we call the trial of our faith is the inevitable result of being alive.

Anon.

Trust in the LORD with all your heart; do not depend on your own understanding. Seek his will in all you do, and he will direct your paths.

Proverbs 3:5–6, NLT

The one who will be found in trial capable of great acts of love, is ever the one who is always doing considerate small ones.

F. W. Robertson, 1816–53

So Christ has now become the High Priest over all the good things that have come. He has entered that great, perfect sanctuary in heaven, not made by human hands and not part of this created world. Once for all time he took blood into that Most Holy Place, but not the blood of goats and calves. He took his own blood, and with it secured our salvation forever.

Under the old system, the blood of goats and bulls and the ashes of a young cow could cleanse people's bodies from ritual defilement. Just think how much more the blood of Christ will purify our hearts from deeds that lead to death so that we can worship the living God. For by the power of the eternal Spirit, Christ offered himself to God as a perfect sacrifice for our sins. That is why he is the one who mediates the new covenant between God and people, so that all who are invited can receive the eternal inheritance God has promised them. For Christ died to set them free from the penalty of the sins they had committed under that first covenant.

Hebrews 9:11–15, NLT

He came once for all time, at the end of the age, to remove the power of sin for ever by his sacrificial death for us.

And just as it is destined that each person dies only once and after that comes judgement, so also Christ died only once as a sacrifice to take away the sins of many people. He will come again but not to deal with our sins again. This time he will bring salvation to all those who are eagerly waiting for him.

Hebrews 9:26–28, NLT

Like a well-written dramatic masterpiece, the entire history of the Old Testament sacrificial system culminates in this triumphant moment. But instead of the priest shedding the blood of one more bull, goat or lamb in a religious ritual, the Lord spills his own blood. On the cross, Christ accomplished once and for all what ritual sacrifice could only prefigure – the cleansing and rebirth of the human heart. Are you entrusting your soul to the ultimate sacrifice of the living Saviour or to some familiar yet inadequate religious system or ritual?

Footnote on Hebrews 9:26–28 from NLT
Touchpoint Bible

> The road,
> You shall follow it.
> The fun,
> You shall forget it.
> The cup,
> You shall empty it.
> The pain,
> You shall conceal it.
> The truth,
> You shall be told it.
> The end,
> You shall endure it.

Tired
And lonely,
So tired
The heart aches.
Meltwater trickles
Down the rocks,
The fingers are numb,
The knees tremble.
It is now,
Now, that you must not give in.
On the path of the others
Are resting places,
Places in the sun
Where they can meet.
But this
Is your path,
And it is now,
Now, that you must not fail.
Weep
If you can,
Weep,
But do not complain.
The way chose you –
And you must be thankful.

Dag Hammarskjöld

Never forget in the darkness what God has
shown you in the light.

Jim Graham

Never forget in the light what God has shown you in the darkness!

When you get to the end of your rope, tie a knot and hang on.

Anon.

Recently the beloved son of a pastor of our church died. His parents described Simon as being 'differently abled' because he had Down's syndrome. He lived until he was twenty-five and was a blessing to all who knew him.

Keith, Simon's father, said he sometimes goes into his now tidy room and sits on his empty bed and prays for those who have an empty space in their lives. That prayer is a big prayer, because it must include millions of people who live with empty spaces for one reason or another – people who have lost loved ones, for whom life will never be the same again.

But there are many more reasons for those empty spaces than the death of a loved one.

The ultimate measure of a man is not where he stands in moments of comfort and convenience but where he stands at times of challenge and controversy.

Anon.

*F*rom the moment we are born we begin to experience loss and stress. The new baby severed from the umbilical cord and the warmth and security of the mother's womb has to experience the struggles of independence. From then on, mother and child go through barely perceptible mini-bereavements, including the first day at school or even, if the mother returns to work, the first day with the child-minder.

Have you ever lost your car keys or had your purse or wallet snatched? Loss of time, loss of plans, missed appointments all contribute to the anger and frustration of the day. This experience is amplified with loss of health, loss of a relationship, such as a divorce and loss of a loved one through death.

Never is it more important to know the security of a 'life hid with Christ' (Col. 3:3), that we are but travellers on a road which ultimately leads in God's time to eternity.

Character is what you are in the dark.

> Let the Holy Spirit fill and control you. Then you will sing psalms and hymns and spiritual songs among yourselves, making music to the Lord in your hearts. And you will always give thanks for everything to God the Father in the name of our Lord Jesus Christ.

Ephesians 5:18–20, NLT

*I*t is not always possible to thank God for *everything that happens, but it is certainly possible and highly beneficial to thank him* in *everything.* Praise works!

> Take up thy cross, the Saviour said
> If thou wouldst my disciple be
> Deny thyself, the world forsake
> And humbly follow after me.
>
> To thee Great Lord the one in three
> All praise forever more ascend;
> O grant us in our home to see
> The heavenly life that knows no end.
>
> *C. W. Everest, 1814–77*

Always do right. This will gratify some people and astonish the rest!

> *Mark Twain, 1835–1910*

Let the words of my mouth, and the meditation of my heart, be acceptable in thy sight, O LORD, my strength, and my redeemer.

> *Psalm 19:14, AV*

The thoughts that in our hearts keep place,
Lord, make a holy, heavenly throng,
And steep in innocence and grace
The issue of each guarded tongue.

T. H. Gill

I heard a story of a little girl in the Far East who had witnessed the brutal murder of her mother by her father, who had then taken his own life. She was adopted into the home of a Christian family. When she went to Sunday school for the first time, the Sunday-school teacher was warned about what had happened.

During the morning, the teacher held up a picture of Jesus. 'Who's that?' she asked.

Immediately the child put her hand up and said wistfully, 'That's the man who was looking after me when my daddy killed my mummy.'

What a wonderful illustration of the God who promises he will never leave or forsake us.

YE ARE NOT YOUR OWN

'Know ye not that ye are not your own?'

There is no such thing as a private life – 'a world within the world' – for a man or woman who is brought into fellowship with Jesus Christ's sufferings. God breaks up the private life of His saints, and makes it a thoroughfare for the world on the one hand and for Himself on the other. No human being can stand that unless he is identified with Jesus Christ. We are not sanctified for ourselves, we are called into the fellowship of the Gospel, and things happen which have nothing to do with us, God is getting us into fellowship with Himself. Let Him have His way, if you do not, instead of being of the slightest use to God in His Redemptive work in the world, you will be a hindrance and a clog.

The first thing God does with us is to get us based on rugged Reality until we do not care what becomes of us individually as long as He gets His way for the purpose of His Redemption. Why shouldn't we go through heartbreaks? Through these doorways God is opening up ways of fellowship with His Son. Most of us fall and collapse at the first grip of pain; we sit down on the threshold of God's purpose and die away of self-pity, and all so-called Christian sympathy will aid us to our death bed. But God will not. He comes with the grip of the pierced hand of His

171

Son. – 'Enter into fellowship with Me; Arise and shine.' If through a broken heart God can bring His purposes to pass in the world, then thank Him for breaking your heart.

Oswald Chambers, 1874–1917

*J*esus wants to transform every kind of human suffering into triumph. He is the only one who can bring life out of death. Every event of our lives provides us with an opportunity to learn life's deepest lessons.

I have heard people argue, 'Ah, but my problem's different, it'll never work for me.' No person's problem is so exclusive that there is no answer. God has not abandoned us. He still cares for us and he will see us through if we trust him.

I am willing to endure anything if it will bring salvation and eternal glory in Christ Jesus to those God has chosen.

2 Timothy 2:10, NLT

I just want to praise You,
Lift my hands and say: 'I love You.'
You are everything to me
And I exalt Your holy name on high.

Arthur Tannous

The main thing about Christianity is not the work we do, but the relationship we maintain and the atmosphere produced by that relationship. That is all God asks us to look after, and it is one thing that is being continually assailed.

Oswald Chambers, 1874–1917

Outward show is a poor substitute for inner worth.

Anon.

Questions to ponder

※ ※ ※

1 How far are you willing to follow Jesus when he said to his Father, 'I want your will, not mine'?

2 Are you willing to let go of your plans for your life if God shows you he has other plans?

3 Do you have selective hearing? Do you say, 'So far but no further'?

4 If the safest place to be is in the centre of God's will, why are you anxious?

5 Check out some Bible verses which will encourage you to stay close to God in times of suffering.

Psalm 22
Psalm 91
Psalm 126
John 3:16
Romans 8:17–18
Hebrews 2:18
2 Corinthians 1:3–5

October

* * *

*T*his is the month when we in the United Kingdom say goodbye to British Summer Time, put our clocks back one hour to Greenwich Mean Time and face the prospect of short days and long winter nights.

I am not a SAD (seasonal adjustment disorder) sufferer – I think I am too busy to allow it to affect me – but I confess to counting down to the shortest day and then rejoicing that the longer days are coming!

I love the long, lazy days of summer when the daylight and open windows allow the balmy warm air to invade the house until almost bedtime. But I make the choice in the winter months to draw the curtains to make my home cosy and give thanks that I have all the facilities to keep myself warm and comfortable.

In all circumstances we have a choice of how we deal with life's issues.

This month we are dealing with the pain of a broken heart. There are few who will go through life without painful problems. We all have experiences that break our hearts and we think we will never smile again, but we do. The question is, how do we handle them?

Do we fill ourselves with self-pity and live as victims for what remains of our lives? Or do we learn from our experience and use it to help and serve others, moving forward with our security in the Lord, rather than behind the excuses of our circumstances?

The choice is ours ...

CHAPTER TEN

Take my (breaking) heart, it is Thine own

It shall be Thy royal throne

✳ ✳ ✳

*N*otice I've added the word 'breaking' into the line above. The reason for this is that we have to be far more creative in coping with heartbreaking experiences than we do if our hearts are singing with happiness!

Jesus understands our pain. Isaiah prophesied this.

> He was despised and rejected – a man of sorrows, acquainted with the bitterest grief. We turned our back on him and looked the other way when he went by. He was despised and we did not care.

Isaiah 53:3, NLT

Most of us experience painful rejection some-time in our lives. It may be the loneliness of relational failure, the esteem-shattering experience of job termination, or the self-condemnation of a guilty conscience. Since we feel rejected by others and sometimes reject ourselves, we often assume that God rejects us as well. In this passage, the prophet anticipates the rejection Jesus would suffer on our behalf. Christ knows not only all the rejection of human life but also the rejection and pain of the cross itself. We can take great hope and comfort in knowing that Jesus understands and feels our rejection. He went to the cross so that we could always know the acceptance and love of God.

Comment from NLT Touchpoint Bible
on rejection

'I want you to know what will happen to the Christians who have died so you will not be full of sorrow like people who have no hope.'

Paul to the Thessalonians (1 Thess. 4:13)

God ... will wipe away all tears.

Revelation 21:4, GNB

Don't be afraid, for I am with you. Do not be dismayed, for I am your God. I will strengthen you. I will help you. I will uphold you with my victorious right hand.

Isaiah 41:10, NLT

Language has created the word loneliness to explain the pain of being alone and the word solitude to explain the glory of being alone.

Paul Tillich, 1886–1965

*T*here is a vast difference between being alone and being lonely. Loneliness is very much a symptom of the society in which we live today. You don't have to be alone to be lonely. Some of our big cities can be the loneliest places to be. The population is so great and housing so costly that hundreds of people can live in bed-sits and flats in one small street and no one has time to communicate with neighbours.

Modern technology has contributed to this. Automatic washing machines, microwaves and computers enable a person to be almost totally isolated within the four walls of the home. The need for communication becomes obsolete. And yet we were made for relationships; to interact with one another. This lack of communication with others is one of the major factors of depression. When a person constantly looks inwards at their own problems and ceases to look outwards towards the needs of others, depression is often the result.

Up to and just beyond the Second World War, families were the bedrock of our society. They lived in the same towns and villages and even streets for generations. There was a real sense of community and belonging. Travel was not as easy, package holidays were unheard of and generally people lived within walking distance or a bus ride from work. In many cases, Grandma lived next door, so that she could give advice based on a lifetime's experience. Grandparents were revered and were also useful for looking after grandchildren. Most of my husband's large family lived in the same village. Everyone knew everyone's business, which possibly was the downside, but people supported one another through adversity and struggles.

THE WORST DISEASE

I have come more and more to realise that being unwanted is the worst disease that any human being can ever experience.

Nowadays we have found medicine for leprosy and lepers can be cured. There is medicine for TB and consumption can be cured. But for being unwanted, except there are willing hands to serve and there's a loving heart to love, I don't think this terrible disease can be cured.

Mother Teresa of Calcutta, 1910–97

Charles Swindoll in his book Seasons of Life *comments that elevators are microcosms of our world today – a large impersonal institution where anonymity, isolation and independence are the uniform of the day. Although you're crammed into a small space with loads of people, no one speaks and no one looks at anybody.*

Strange! People who are all about the same height and speak the same language are suddenly as silent as a roomful of nuns when they occupy common space.

It's almost as if there's an official sign that reads 'No talking, no smiling, no touching and no eye contact allowed without written consent of the management.'

No exceptions!

A basic quality of our healthy social lives is being eroded, is being diluted, distorted and demeaned by the elevator mentality.

Charles Swindoll

He goes on to quote Dr Philip Zimbardo from an article in Psychology Today:

> I know of no more potent killer than isolation. There is no more destructive influence on physical and mental health than the isolation of you from me and us from them. It has been shown to be a central agent in the etiology of depression, paranoia, schizophrenia, rape, suicide, mass murder ...
>
> The devil's strategy for our times is to trivialise a human existence in a number of ways: by isolating us from one another while creating the delusion that the reasons are time pressures, work demands or anxieties created by economic uncertainty; by fostering narcissism and the fierce competition to be No. 1.
>
> *Dr Philip Zimbardo*

The following monologue was written by Gloria Storm, Nosmo King and Ernest Longstaffe in 1937. It was performed by Nosmo King (a stage name derived from 'No Smoking'), who invariably ended his humorous stage or radio acts with a serious monologue.

LOYALTY

Never believe the worst of a man,
When once you have seen his best,
Of any loyalty worth the name,
This is the surest test.
Gossip is ready at every turn,
Your faith and trust to slay,
But the loyal soul is deaf to doubt,
Whatever the world may say.
Whatever you hear on others' lips,
Don't let it spoil your own,
Let your faith still stronger be,
While the seed of slander's sown.
Keep the image before your eyes,
Of the friend who's a friend to you,
And stand by that friend through thick
    and thin,
Whatever the world may do.
Never believe the worst of a man,
When our own soul sees the best,
All that matters is what you know,
Not what the others have guessed.
And if all you know is straight and fine,
And has brought you friendship's joys,
Be proud to treasure the truth that's
    yours,
Whatever the world destroys.

A young woman went to speak to a counsellor because she was so lonely and needed a friend, but couldn't find anybody who would befriend her. The counsellor asked her what qualities she would want to find in a friend. She named some of the qualities she thought would make a special friend. The counsellor, with great wisdom, replied. 'Then go and be that person to someone else.'

> To handle yourself use your head
> To handle others use your heart.

> *Anon.*

The will of God will never take you where his grace cannot keep you.

> *Anon.*

When they were discouraged, I smiled at them. My look of approval was precious to them.

> *Job 29:24, NLT*

I f you expect anybody but the Lord to meet all your needs you will always be disappointed.

There is only one Being who loves you perfectly, and that is God, yet the New Testament distinctly states that we are to love as God does; so the first step is obvious. If ever we are going to have perfect love in our hearts we must have the very nature of God in us.

Oswald Chambers, 1874–1917

Four things a man must learn to do
If he would make his record true
To think without confusion clearly
To love his fellow man sincerely
To act from honest motives purely
To trust God and Heaven securely.

Henry Van Dyke, 1852–1933

People don't care how much you know, till they know how much you care.

Anon.

BEATITUDES
FOR THOSE WHO COMFORT

Blessed are those who do not use tears to measure
the true feelings of *others*.

Blessed are those who stifle the urge to say, 'I
understand' – when they don't.

Blessed are those who do not expect the bereaved
to put into the past someone who is still
fresh in their hearts.

Blessed are those who do not always have a quick
'comforting' answer.

Blessed are those who do not make judgments on
another's closeness to God by their reaction
to the loss of a loved one.

Blessed are those who hear with their hearts and
not with their minds.

Blessed are those who allow the sorrowing
enough time to heal.

Blessed are those who admit their discomfort and
put it aside to help others.

Blessed are those who do not give unwanted advice.

Blessed are those who continue to call, visit and
reach out when the crowd has dwindled and
the wounded are left standing alone.

Blessed are those who know the worth of each
person as a unique individual and do not
pretend that they can be replaced or
forgotten.

Blessed are those who realise the fragility of
sorrow and handle it with an understanding
shoulder and a loving heart.

Anon.

If you live in hope you live in pain. If you have a strong and enduring hope that Christ will be placed back at the centre of public life, you are in pain. If you long to see your entire neighbourhood reached for the gospel and growing numbers responding to Christ, you are in pain. And if you are aware that there is little strategy in place for any of this to be realised (vision without strategy turns sour) I know you are in pain. But our hope is with those who carry such pain. Thank God for the body of Christ – it was one of his very best ideas. And thank God for the pain that makes us aware of our need of others: it helps us live with a little more humility and helps us to fulfil the great prayer of Jesus which John records in the 17th chapter of his narrative.

I don't like pain, I like to create a cushion around myself to protect me from pain. And the notion of suffering is not one that fills me with joy or vibrant expectancy. But this is where my natural inclinations, cowardice and fears need to come in line with scripture as I live out my life in the present and prepare for the future.

Gerald Coates

This is the true joy in life, the being used for a purpose recognised by yourself as a mighty one; the being thoroughly worn out before you are thrown on the scrap heap; the being a force of Nature instead of a feverish selfish little clod of ailments and grievances complaining that the world will not devote itself to making you happy.

George Bernard Shaw, 1856–1950

Small kindnesses, small courtesies, small considerations, habitually practised in our social intercourse, give a greater charm to the character than the display of great talents and accomplishments.

M. A. Kelty

What lies behind us and what lies before us are tiny matters compared with what lies within us.

Ralph Waldo Emerson, 1803–82

I look for someone to come and help me,
but no one gives me a passing thought!
No one will help me;
no one cares a bit what happens to me.
Then I pray to you, O LORD.
I say, 'You are my place of refuge.
You are all I really want in life.
Hear my cry, for I am very low.'

Psalm 142:4–6, NLT

*I*n my own case I decided I had a choice. I could either be miserable because people were not caring enough and therefore not meeting all my needs, or I could choose to be cheerful and save my tears for the bedroom behind closed doors. I realised I didn't need to burden anyone else with my grief – it was between me and God only. My friends were very important to me and I didn't want them to reject me because of my constant misery!

Tears are proof of love
The more love, the more tears
If this be true, then how could
we ask that the pain cease
Altogether?
For then the memory of love would go with it
The pain of grief is the price we pay for love.

Anon.

I was told about a man who had suffered from depression for a long time. He had confounded all the efforts of his psychiatrist to cure him. One day, as a last resort, the psychiatrist asked him a question. 'Is there anybody in your life who really helped and encouraged you?' The man thought for a moment and said, 'Yes – a teacher.'

'Right,' said the psychiatrist. 'Find out his address and write to him and thank him for the way he encouraged you.' The man did this and sometime later he received a reply from this now elderly teacher.

'Thank you so much for your kind letter,' he said. 'In all my years of teaching, yours is the only letter of appreciation I have ever received.'

The man was so shocked when he read this letter that he began to make a list of all the people in his life he was grateful to, both known and unknown, including writers, journalists, royalty and so on. He wrote over five hundred letters and never suffered from depression again!

We can be so self-obsessed that we fail to reap the joys and pleasures of being with and reaching out to others.

> There are 'friends' who destroy each other,
> but a real friend sticks closer than a brother.
>
> *Proverbs 18:24, NLT*

I bow my knee before your throne,
I know my life is not my own
I offer up a song of praise
To bring you pleasure Lord

I seek the giver, not the gift
My heart's desire is to lift you
High above all earthly kings
To bring you pleasure Lord

Hallelujah, Hallelujah
Hallelujah, Glory to the King.

Bonnie Deuschle

What the caterpillar calls the end of the world,
the Creator calls a butterfly.

Anon.

God was very gracious to me and showed me very early on how to avoid self-pity. About two weeks after Roy's death, I was flying home from Belfast after a TV chat show to promote his autobiography. As I arrived at Heathrow and walked down the corridor towards the concourse where the taxi drivers wait with placards for their 'pick-ups', I watched the young woman ahead of me greet a waiting man and melt into his arms! I burst into tears on the spot and just sobbed and sobbed. (It's normally when you leave *on a journey that you cry – not when you* arrive!)

'I haven't anyone to meet me any more,' I thought. 'I haven't any arms to enfold me … I have to make my way to the bus to the long-term car park, find my car and make my way home to an empty house.' Poor old me! *I suddenly realised what I was doing! Self-pity for* me *was the slippery slope to depression. I was determined not to go down that road. I had been there before and didn't like it! From that moment I resolutely refused myself any tears of self-pity. 'What are you up to?' I said. 'Pull yourself together. You have no cause for complaint. You had thirty-one years with a wonderful man who cared for you. Now you are on your own. Be grateful for all you* do *have. You have a car with petrol in it and a home to go to. So get on that bus and stop complaining!' It worked! Of course there were many tears of sadness, but by being cheerful, I avoided the loneliness of being shunned by friends.*

Decide to sing!

Loneliness for me as a widow is:

1 *Having to enter a room full of people – alone.*

2 *Having to take sole responsibility for all the 'things' that go wrong in my life.*

3 *Coming home after an exciting or special day and having no one to share it with.*

4 *Hearing a special song on the radio and not being able to relive the memory of it together.*

5 *Special moments with grandchildren alone.*

The best time to be happy is *now*.
The best place to be happy is *here*.

Anon.

I am not alone
   by night
   or by day,
Or by circumstance
Neither in the silence
Nor in the city's roar;
   Nor as I lie
At the door of death,
Or stand on the threshold
   of a new life;
For thou art with me
Around me
Underneath me,
Bearing me up
Giving me strength
   Calling me on
   I am not alone
   Thou hast been
   Thou wilt be,
   Thou art with me
Lo, I am always in thy care.
Amen.

Samuel F. Pugh

Measure thy life by loss and not by gain: not
by wine drunk but by the wine poured forth,
for love's strength standeth in love's sacrifice,
he that suffereth most hath most to give.

Ugo Bassi

It is easy to cause our own isolation without realising it – through time pressures, work demands,
anxieties with family members, money problems –
believing they are very valid reasons for not getting in
touch with others. We need to maintain contact with
those we love, even in these difficult times, either
through a phone call or a card with a promise or an
IOU or a date in the diary even a few months ahead. I
know how important this is, because I'm guilty myself
of becoming so busy that social life goes onto the
back burner. I try now to make a date in the diary
when I phone people or my reply will always be – 'We
must get together soon' – and then another year goes
by!

True friendships are bonded by loyalty and
commitment and strengthen in adversity.

Anon.

Help us to help each other, Lord,
Each other's cross to bear.
Let each his friendly aid afford
And feel each other's care.

Help us to build each other up,
Our little stock improve.
Increase our faith, confirm our hope
And perfect us in love.

Charles Wesley, 1707–88

We also need to be reminded to appreciate the people who have helped and encouraged us through our lives and to make sure we thank them before it's too late. Think of the people who have made a difference – a teacher, a parent, a grandparent, a friend – people who have been good role models for you. How much better to say thank you in their lifetime than to their loved ones once they have died.

It is good to say, 'Thank you' to the Lord, to sing praises to the God who is above all gods. Every morning tell him, 'Thank you for your kindness,' and every evening rejoice in all his faithfulness.

Psalm 92:1–2, LB

I will offer up my life in spirit and truth
Pouring out the oil of love as my worship to
    You.
In surrender I must give my every part;
Lord, receive the sacrifice of a broken heart.

> *Jesus, what can I give,*
> *What can I bring*
> *To so faithful a friend,*
> *To so loving a king?*
> *Saviour, what can be said?*
> *What can be sung*
> *As a praise of Your name*
> *For the things You have done?*
> *Oh, my words could not tell,*
> *Not even in part,*
> *Of the debt of love that is owed*
> *By this thankful heart.*

You deserve my every breath, for you've
    paid the great cost;
Giving up Your life to death, even death on
    a cross.
You took all my shame away, there defeated
    my sin,
Opened up the gates of heaven and have
    beckoned me in.

> *Jesus, what can I give …*

Matt Redman

Questions to ponder

❋ ❋ ❋

1 *Where does your security lie?*

2 *Is your life and its circumstances founded on your position and material assets? Or are your material assets and position based on your faith in God through Jesus? If it is the latter, it will remain firm through life's storms and sorrows, like the house that was built on solid rock.*

3 *How could God use the painful experiences in your own life to help others in similar circumstances?*

4 *Who could be more useful in the support of another, than one who has personally experienced their pain? Don't hide those experiences – use them.*

5 *How can you change your attitude from one of self-pity to one of gratitude and praise?*

6 *Are you prepared to begin that change today?*

7 *Use a notebook to remind you each time you achieved this change and the difference it made.*

November

Just one look across the many rows of magazines in the newsagent's will remind you of all that lies ahead in order that you might have a perfect Christmas!

You will be saying things like, 'Where has the year gone? It seems like only last week that I took the decorations down and I haven't even started to think of a present list!'

All the magazines point out ways in which we can cook a perfect turkey, decorate a perfect tree and wrap a perfect present! They show us ways to look wonderful. All these ideas are to impress others, but it is all external and says nothing about how we are feeling on the inside.

I heard someone speaking about the many funeral services he had conducted. Among the varied eulogies given about the deceased, he had never heard mention of the amount of money accrued, the size of the house, the expensive, elegant clothes or the exotic holidays taken. No, the comments were only about how those people had loved and cared for others. The difference they had made to communities and to people's lives. In other words – love is what lasts.

CHAPTER ELEVEN

Take my love; my Lord, I pour

At Thy feet its treasure store

✳ ✳ ✳

*L*oving when you least feel like it, and when those you love least deserve it, is loving the way God loves.

There are those we find easy to love – we think the same way, enjoy the same sense of humour and have similar lifestyles. But then there are those who seem to be all elbows. The chemistry just isn't right between us. In our experience they are just plain difficult and the less we see them the better! But that's not God's way.

His love is patient and kind. It doesn't envy others or boast. His love isn't proud or rude or self-seeking, neither is it easily angered. He keeps no record of wrongs. His love rejoices in truth, not evil. His love protects, trusts, hopes and always perseveres (taken from I Cor. 13).

Does yours?

You must love the Lord your God with all your heart, all your soul, all your mind, and all your strength.

Mark 12:30, NLT

Love for the Lord is not an ethereal, intellectual, dream-like thing. It is the intensest, the most vital, the most passionate love of which the human heart is capable.

Oswald Chambers, 1874–1917

When you obey me, you remain in my love … I have told you this so that you will be filled with my joy. Yes, your joy will overflow!

John 15:10–11, NLT

I find doing the will of God leaves me no time for disputing about His plans.

George MacDonald, 1824–1905

Lord it is my chief complaint,
That my love is weak and faint.
Yet I love thee and adore
O for grace to love thee more.

William Cowper, 1731–1800

Real love begins when nothing is expected in return.

Antoine de Saint-Exupéry

Whatsoever a man soweth, that shall he also reap.

Galatians 6:7, AV

The life above, when this is past,
Is the ripe fruit of life below.

Sow love, and taste its fruitage pure;
Sow peace, and reap its harvest bright
Sow sunbeams on the rock and moor,
And find a harvest-home of light.

Horatius Bonar

Let your lives overflow with thanksgiving for all he has done.

Colossians 2:7, NLT

When Roy was told he had lung cancer and was given three months to live, it was a tremendous shock to both of us. For about twenty-four hours I cried every time I tried to speak to him. However, one thing quickly became evident. Sadness was the only emotion we were experiencing. There was no anger, no remorse, simply sadness because the strong and loving relationship we had known for so long might not continue for much longer. I suddenly realised what a privileged position we were in. Roy had had a great life. He had made the most of every opportunity he had been given. We were both so grateful for all we had. Most of all, we recognised the importance of good relationships. When I became a Christian many years before, our marriage changed and became stronger than it had ever been. If that had not happened, I would have been filled with remorse for not being a better wife, giving him more time, listening to his problems, caring more ... the list of regrets would have been endless. But there was none of that, and the only emotion we needed to display was sadness that the relationship we had might be coming to an end.

> How many go forth in the morning
> Who never come home at night?
> And hearts are broken
> For harsh words spoken
> That sorrow can never put right.
> We have careful words for the stranger
> And smiles for the sometime guest

But for our own, the bitter tone ...
Though we love our own the best!

Anon.

Love is a fabric that never fades, no matter
how often it is washed in the waters of
adversity and grief.

Anon.

*T*hink of people whose loved ones died without
warning – a heart attack, an accident, a stroke.
There would have been no time to say goodbye, no
time to put the wrong things right, to say, 'Sorry',
'Thank you', 'I appreciate you'. How vital it is to keep
short accounts so that we don't live with remorse.

Life is not a holiday but an education. And
the eternal lesson for us all is how better we
can love.

Henry Drummond, 1851–97

Let me not to the marriage of true minds
Admit impediments. Love is not love
Which alters when it alteration finds,
Or bends with the remover to remove.
O, no! it is an ever-fixed mark,
That looks on tempests and is never shaken;
It's the star to every wand'ring bark,
Whose worth's unknown, although his
        height be taken
Love's not Time's fool, though rosy lips
        and cheeks
Within his bending sickle's compass come;
Love alters not with his brief hours and
        weeks,
But bears it out even to the edge of doom.
If this be error, and upon me prov'd,
I never writ, nor no man ever lov'd.

William Shakespeare, 1564–1616

We ought to love our maker for his own
sake, without either hope of good or fear
of pain.

Anon.

And may the Lord make your love grow and
overflow to each other and to everyone else,
just as our love overflows towards you.

1 Thessalonians 3:12, NLT

Consider Jesus Christ in every person, and in ourselves, Jesus Christ as father in his father, Jesus Christ as brother in his brothers, Jesus Christ as poor in the poor, Jesus Christ as rich in the rich, Jesus Christ as priest and doctor in priests, Jesus Christ as sovereign in princes. For by his glory he is everything that is great being God, and by his mortal life he is everything that is wretched and abject. That is why he took on this unhappy condition, so that he could be in every person and a model for every condition of men.

Blaise Pascal, 1623–62

Why, when Jesus rose from the dead, had God not completely healed him by removing all his scars?

It was identification.

When we bear the scars of our lives, are people more able to identify with us? If so, why are we afraid of being wounded?

He was wounded and crushed for our sins. He was beaten that we might have peace. He was whipped, and we were healed!

Isaiah 53:5, NLT

MY DAYS GO ON

I praise thee while my days go on;
I love thee while my days go on:
Through dark and dearth, through fire and frost,
With emptied arms and treasure lost,
I thank thee while my days go on.

Anon.

THE ALTAR

A broken altar, Lord, thy servant rears,
Made of a heart and cemented with tears;
    Whose parts are as thy hand did frame;
    No workman's tool hath touched the same.

        A heart alone
        Is such a stone
        As nothing but
        Thy power doth cut.
        Wherefore each part
        Of my hard heart
        Meets in this frame
        To praise thy name;

That if I chance to hold my peace,
    These stones to praise thee may not cease,
Oh, let thy blessed sacrifice be mine,
And sanctify this altar to be thine.

George Herbert, 1593–1633

And God has given us his Spirit as proof that we live in him and he in us. Furthermore, we have seen with our own eyes and now testify that the Father sent his Son to be the Saviour of the world. All who proclaim that Jesus is the Son of God have God living in them, and they live in God. We know how much God loves us, and we have put our trust in him.

God is love, and all who live in love live in God, and God lives in them. And as we live in God, our love grows more perfect. So we will not be afraid on the day of judgement, but we can face him with confidence because we are like Christ here in this world.

Such love has no fear because perfect love expels all fear. If we are afraid, it is for fear of judgement, and this shows that his love has not been perfected in us. We love each other as a result of his loving us first.

If someone says, 'I love God,' but hates a Christian brother or sister, that person is a liar; for if we don't love people we can see, how can we love God, whom we have not seen: And God himself has commanded that we must love not only him but our Christian brothers and sisters, too.

1 John 4:13–21, NLT

I love You, Lord, and I lift my voice
To worship You, O my soul rejoice!
Take joy, my King, in what You hear,
May it be a sweet, sweet sound in Your ear.

Laurie Klein

Questions to ponder

❃ ❃ ❃

1 *Are you more concerned with what people think of you than what God thinks of you?*

2 *Are you prepared to go on loving without expecting a response?*

3 *Jesus said that the two most important commands were to love God and to love your neighbour as yourself. Love is a commitment. It is not dependent on the feel-good factor, but on a conscious decision to expend yourself for the wellbeing of another; to put others' interests before your own. Jesus gave us the perfect example when he gave his own life to save us. Is the world a better place because you have been in it?*

4 *What is the legacy of your life which will be remembered at your funeral?*

December

I don't need to remind anyone of the stress and *pressure and busyness of this time of year! But it doesn't have to be like that. Jesus arrived in abject poverty and humility with none of the ceremony normally afforded to kings and princes. Yet we get so caught up with the trappings of Christmas, we forget the beauty of his simplicity.*

Maybe this 'Christbirthday' can be different as we refuse to allow the world's demands to take hold of us and we discover afresh his purpose for our lives.

An uncle of mine sent the following to me many years ago. He must have realised I needed it and I am still learning the lesson!

Humility is perfect quietness of heart. It is to have no trouble, never to be fretted, irritated, sore or disappointed. It is to expect nothing, to wonder at nothing that is done to me. It is to be at rest when nobody praises me and when I am blamed or despised. It is to have a blessed home in the Lord where I can go in and shut the door and kneel to my Father in secret and am at peace as in a deep sea of calmness when all around and above is trouble.

Andrew Murray, 1828–1917

*A*re you willing to put this lesson into practice this month?

CHAPTER TWELVE

Take my 'self', and I will be

Ever, only, all, for Thee

✳ ✳ ✳

*H*uman beings are 'self'-ish creatures.

It is the divisive force threatening every relationship, the weakness allowing healthy pursuits to become destructive obsessions and the dark force behind all sin. It is not anger, pride, hatred or malice – although it can be in all four. It is simple, everyday, garden-variety selfishness. From Adam and Eve, who ate of the forbidden tree because they desired knowledge reserved only for God, to Judas who betrayed his Lord for thirty pieces of silver, the Bible warns of the seductive power of selfishness. Fortunately Scripture also leads us to Jesus Christ, the one whose redemptive work could transform selfishness to unselfishness.

Anon.

Don't be selfish; don't live to make a good impression on others. Be humble, thinking of others as better than yourself.

Philippians 2:3, NLT

If you try to keep your life for yourself, you will lose it.

Matthew 16:25, NLT

The more you think of yourself, the harder it is to find eternal life.

Our behaviour is a revelation of our character. It is the sum total of all that distinguishes us as a unique person. As opposed to personality which may be put on like a mask to suit the mood of the moment, character grows out of who we really are and what we desire to become. Many of us strive for excellence in our intellect, by gaining degrees or business and financial acumen, but this does not necessarily describe our character. Many people have arrived at the top of their particular ladders without scruples, but moral excellence is the main indication of good character. To know and follow Jesus' example of love, kindness, gentleness and integrity is the indication of godly character.

As the Spirit of the Lord works within us, we become more and more like him.

2 Corinthians 3:18, NLT

It would be interesting, certainly educational and possibly alarming if everything people said about us in our absence was written down for all to read.

How long is it going to take God to free us from the morbid habit of thinking about ourselves? We must get sick unto death of ourselves, until there is no longer any surprise at anything God can tell us about ourselves. We cannot touch the depths of meanness in ourselves. There is only one place where we are right, and that is in Christ Jesus. When we are there, we have to pour out for all we are worth in the ministry of the interior.

Oswald Chambers, 1874–1917

True worship is not self-centred or a self-indulgent expression of our tastes, but takes my eyes off me and it is my choice, however things are in my life, to give God pleasure.

I WANT TO KNOW CHRIST

I know that I know that my life is redeemed
I know I have found what some only have
    dreamed
I hold in my heart the pearl of great price
Dear God hear my cry – I want to know Christ

I want to know Christ
I keep him before me
I lift up my eyes
I drink in His glory
I press toward the goal
His goodness unfolds
March on O my soul
I want to know Christ

I know that my path is the way of the cross
So I count what I've gained and forget what
    I've lost
In pain there is joy – in death there is life
Dear God, hear my cry – I want to know Christ

And the things that entangle me
I lay them down
All the treasures and trophies of life
Oh let them be lost
Only let me be found in Christ.

Michael Hudson and Gary Diskell

I have known criticism, sometimes quite justified, which I have had to accept, but I have also been the scapegoat for other people's failings, which is much harder to deal with. Everything inside me cries out for justice. 'It's not fair – it's not true – I'm not to blame!'

Then God has to speak quietly into my heart. 'I know the truth, you know the truth, the rest does not matter.'

The result? Peace.

God knows my side, the other person's side and his side and he still loves me.

You can justify your every action, but God looks at your motives.

Proverbs 21:2

My obligation is to do the right thing. The rest is in God's hands.

Martin Luther King, 1929–68

Never let loyalty and kindness get away from you! Wear them like a necklace; write them deep within your heart.

Proverbs 3:3, NLT

I don't know the key to success, but the key to failure is to try to please everyone.

Bill Cosby

It is quite possible for any man among us to get to a place where there is no such thing as truth or purity and no man gets there without himself being to blame … no man can do wrong in his heart and see right afterwards. If I am going to approach Holy Ground I must get into the right frame of mind – the excellency of a broken heart.

Oswald Chambers, 1874–1917

Oh, what a wonderful God we have! How great are his riches and wisdom and knowledge! How impossible it is for us to understand his decisions and his methods! For who can know what the Lord is thinking? Who knows enough to be his counsellor? And who could ever give him so much that he would have to pay it back? for everything comes from him; everything exists by his power and is intended for his glory. To him be glory evermore. Amen.

Romans 11:33–36, NLT

I lift my eyes before your throne
I know my life is not my own
I offer up a song of praise
To bring you pleasure Lord

I seek the given not the gift
My one desire is to lift
You high above all earthly kings
To bring you pleasure Lord.

Alleluya Alleluya Glory to the King

Anon.

If ever human love was tender, and self-sacrificing, and devoted; if ever it could bear and forbear; if ever it could suffer gladly for its loved ones; if ever it was willing to pour itself out in a lavish abandonment for the comfort or pleasure of its objects; then infinitely more is Divine love tender, and self-sacrificing, and devoted, and glad to bear and forbear, and to suffer, and to lavish its best of gifts and blessings upon the objects of its love. Put together all the tenderest love you know of, the deepest you have ever felt, and the strongest that has ever been poured out upon you, and heap upon it all the love of all the loving human hearts in the world, and then multiply it by infinity, and you will begin, perhaps, to have some faint glimpse of what the love of God is.

H. W. S.

*I*t is human nature to worry. Some people wouldn't be happy without something to worry about. Jesus tells us that all the worrying we can do will not add a moment to our lives. His teaching is not to worry. Paul tells the Philippians 'Don't worry about anything, instead pray about everything', and Peter's advice is to 'give all your worries to God for he cares about you'.

Many people have to be at their wit's end before they would think of praying and yet as Christians we know it is a first response, not a last resort.

Prayer nourishes the life of Jesus in me and enables me to trust him with all my worries.

Everyone needs something bigger than themselves in a crisis – something to hang on to that will give them confidence that everything will be all right. That's when people might turn to prayer, or religion or tarot cards or horoscopes.

However, if we make a habit of prayer whatever our circumstances, when the crisis comes, it is our first response.

It took terrifying affliction in the life of Aleksandr Solzhenitsyn to enable him to find truth and reality.

It was only when I lay there on rotting prison straw that I sensed within myself the first stirring of good. Gradually, it was disclosed to me that the line separating good and evil passes, not through states, nor between classes, nor between political parties either, but right through all human hearts. So bless you, prison, for having been in my life.

> *Aleksandr Solzhenitsyn,*
> *quoted by Philip Yancey*

When I refused to confess my sin,
I was weak and miserable,
and I groaned all day long.
Day and night your hand of
    discipline was heavy on me.
My strength evaporated like water
    in the summer heat.
Finally I confessed all my sins to
    you
and stopped trying to hide them.
I said to myself, 'I will confess my
    rebellion to the LORD'.
And you forgave me! All my guilt is
    gone.

> *Psalm 32:3–5, NLT*

I ask not, 'Take away this weight of care';
No, for that love I pray that all can bear,
And for the faith that whatso'er befall
Must needs be good, and for my profit prove,
Since from my Father's heart most rich in love,
And from His bounteous hands it cometh all.

C. J. P. Spitta

Be like the promontory, against which the waves continually break; but it stands firm, and tames the fury of the water around it. Unhappy am I, because this has happened to me? Not so, but happy am I, though this has happened to me, because I continue free from pain, neither crushed by the present, nor fearing the future. Will then this which has happened prevent thee from being just, magnanimous, temperate, prudent, secure against the inconsiderate opinions and falsehood? Remember, too, on every occasion which leads thee to vexation to apply this principle: that this is not a misfortune, but that to bear it nobly is good fortune.

Marcus Antonius, c.83–30 BC

What a friend we have in Jesus,
All our sins and griefs to bear!
What a privilege to carry
Everything to God in prayer!
O what peace we often forfeit,
O what needless pain we bear –
All because we do not carry
Everything to God in prayer!

Have we trials and temptations?
Is there trouble anywhere?
We should never be discouraged:
Take it to the Lord in prayer!
Can we find a friend so faithful,
Who will all our sorrows share?
Jesus knows our every weakness –
Take it to the Lord in prayer!

Are we weak and heavy-laden,
Cumbered with a load of care?
Jesus is our only refuge
Take it to the Lord in prayer!
Do thy friends despise, forsake thee?
Take it to the Lord in prayer!
In His arms He'll take and shield thee,
Thou wilt find a solace there.

Joseph Medlicott Scriven, 1819–86

*P*rayer is not a one-way telephone conversation to God telling him our needs, but also involves listening to what God has to say to us. It provides us with a unique and necessary opportunity to have a personal relationship with a God who cares about us. Our trust and belief in Jesus and what he did for us – through his death … he opened the way to the Father – is fundamental to every prayer we pray.

> Always be joyful. Keep on praying. No matter what happens, always be thankful, for this is God's will for you who belong to Christ Jesus.

1 Thessalonians 5:16–18, NLT

My Jesus, I love Thee, I know Thou art mine,
for Thee all the pleasures of sin I resign;
my gracious Redeemer, my Saviour art Thou,
if ever I loved Thee, my Jesus, 'tis now.

I love Thee because Thou hast first lovèd me,
and purchased my pardon on Calvary's tree;
I love Thee for wearing the thorns on Thy brow,
if ever I loved Thee, my Jesus, 'tis now.

I'll love Thee in life, I will love Thee in death,
and praise Thee as long as Thou lendest me breath;
and say, when the death-dew lies cold on my brow:
if ever I loved Thee, my Jesus, 'tis now.

In mansions of glory and endless delight,
I'll ever adore Thee and dwell in Thy sight;
I'll sing with the glittering crown on my brow:
if ever I loved Thee, my Jesus, 'tis now.

W. R. Featherstone, 1846–73

I see myself now at the end of my Journey, my toilsome days are ended. I am going now to see that Head that was Crowned with Thorns, and that Face that was spit upon for me.

I have formerly lived by hear-say and Faith, but now I go where I shall live by sight and shall be with Him in whose company I delight myself. I have loved to hear my Lord spoken of, and wherever I have seen the print of His shoe in the earth, there I have coveted to set my foot too. His name has been to me as a Civet Box, yea, sweeter than all perfumes. His voice has been to me most sweet and His countenance, I have desired more than they that have most desired the light of the sun. His word did I use to gather for my food and for antidotes against my faintings. He has held me and I have kept me from mine iniquities. Yea, my steps hath He strengthened in His way.

But glorious it was to see how the open region was filled with horses and chariots, with trumpeters and pipers, with singers and

227

players on stringed instruments to welcome
the pilgrims as they went up and followed
one another in at the beautiful gate of the
city.

John Bunyan, 1628–88, Pilgrim's Progress

To God be the glory! Great things He hath
    done;
So loved He the world that He gave us His
    son;
Who yielded His life an atonement for sin,
And opened the life gate that all may go in.

> *Praise the Lord, praise the Lord!*
> *Let the earth hear His voice;*
> *Praise the Lord, praise the Lord!*
> *Let the people rejoice:*
> *O come to the Father, through*
>   *Jesus the Son*
> *And give Him the glory; great*
>   *things He hath done!*

O perfect redemption, the purchase of blood!
To every believer the promise of God;
The vilest offender who truly believes,
That moment from Jesus a pardon receives.

> *Praise the Lord …*

Great things He hath taught us, great things
     He hath done,
And great our rejoicing through Jesus the
     Son;
But purer, and higher, and greater will be
Our wonder, our rapture, when Jesus we see.

Praise the Lord ...

Frances van Alstyne (Fanny J. Crosby), 1820–1915

Leave the irreparable past in His hands and
step out into the irresistible future with
Him.

Oswald Chambers, 1874–1917

Amen! Blessing and glory and wisdom and
thanksgiving and honour and power and
strength belong to our God for ever and
ever. Amen!

Revelation 7:12, NLT

The chief end of man is to glorify God and
enjoy him for ever.

Shorter Catechism, *1647*

Questions to ponder

❋ ❋ ❋

1 Is your life characterised by the way you care for others or are you taken up by your own desires and needs?

2 What is your motivation for caring for the needy? Is it to obey Jesus' instructions to feed the hungry, give drink to the thirsty, clothe the naked, visit the prisoners (Matt. 25:31–46) or is it to fulfil your own need to be needed and for human affirmation?

3 Are you one who criticises and tears down, or are you committed to encouraging and building up others?

4 As you think of your own lifestyle, how does it help or hinder your walk with God? Do you make time to draw aside to ask him what he wants of your life?

5 As the year draws to a close, how have you changed? What have you heard God say to you? What have you been able to put into practice as a result?

Let my life be a love song to you,
O Lord.

Index of First Lines, Titles and Authors

* * *